T0260982

Praise for *Microservice Architecture*

The authors' approach of starting with a value proposition, "Speed and Safety at Scale and in Harmony," and reasoning from there, is an important contribution to thinking about application design.

—*Mel Conway, Educator and Inventor*

A well-thought-out and well-written description of the organizing principles underlying the microservices architectural style with a pragmatic example of applying them in practice.

—*James Lewis, Principal Consultant, ThoughtWorks*

This book demystifies one of the most important new tools for building robust, scalable software systems at speed.

—*Otto Berkes, Chief Technology Officer, CA Technologies*

If you've heard of companies doing microservices and want to learn more, *Microservice Architecture* is a great place to start. It addresses common questions and concerns about breaking down a monolith and the challenges you'll face with culture, practices, and tooling. The microservices topic is a big one and this book gives you smart pointers on where to go next.

—*Chris Munns, Business Development Manager—DevOps, Amazon Web Services*

Anyone who is building a platform for use inside or outside an organization should read this book. It provides enough "a-ha" insights to keep everyone on your team engaged, from the business sponsor to the most technical team member. Highly recommended!

—*Dave Goldberg, Director, API Products, Capital One*

A practical roadmap to microservices design and the underlying cultural and organizational change that is needed to make it happen successfully.

—*Mark Boyd, Writer/Analyst, Platformable*

An essential guidebook for your microservices journey, presenting the concepts, discussions, and structures supportive of this architectural pattern as well as the pragmatic ground work to become successful.

—*Ian Kelly, Experimenter and Contributor, CA Technologies*

Microservice Architecture
Aligning Principles, Practices, and Culture

Irakli Nadareishvili, Ronnie Mitra,
Matt McLarty, and Mike Amundsen

Beijing · Boston · Farnham · Sebastopol · Tokyo  O'REILLY®

Microservice Architecture

by Irakli Nadareishvili, Ronnie Mitra, Matt McLarty, and Mike Amundsen

Copyright © 2016 Mike Amundsen, Matt McLarty, Ronnie Mitra, Irakli Nadareishvili. All rights reserved.

Printed in the United States of America.

Published by O'Reilly Media, Inc., 1005 Gravenstein Highway North, Sebastopol, CA 95472.

O'Reilly books may be purchased for educational, business, or sales promotional use. Online editions are also available for most titles (*http://safaribooksonline.com*). For more information, contact our corporate/institutional sales department: 800-998-9938 or corporate@oreilly.com .

Editors: Brian MacDonald and Holly Bauer
Production Editor: Kristen Brown
Copyeditor: Christina Edwards
Proofreader: Kim Cofer

Indexer: WordCo Indexing Services, Inc.
Interior Designer: David Futato
Cover Designer: Karen Montgomery
Illustrator: Melanie Yarbrough

June 2016:   First Edition

Revision History for the First Edition
2016-06-02:   First Release
2016-07-18:   Second Release

See *http://oreilly.com/catalog/errata.csp?isbn=9781491956250* for release details.

The O'Reilly logo is a registered trademark of O'Reilly Media, Inc. *Microservice Architecture*, the cover image, and related trade dress are trademarks of O'Reilly Media, Inc.

While the publisher and the authors have used good faith efforts to ensure that the information and instructions contained in this work are accurate, the publisher and the authors disclaim all responsibility for errors or omissions, including without limitation responsibility for damages resulting from the use of or reliance on this work. Use of the information and instructions contained in this work is at your own risk. If any code samples or other technology this work contains or describes is subject to open source licenses or the intellectual property rights of others, it is your responsibility to ensure that your use thereof complies with such licenses and/or rights.

978-1-491-95625-0

[LSI]

Table of Contents

Part II.   Microservice Design Principles

Part III.   Microservices in Practice

Preface

Microservice architecture has emerged as a common pattern of software development from the practices of a number of leading organizations. These practices includes principles, technologies, methodologies, organizational tendencies, and cultural characteristics. Companies taking steps to implement microservices and reap their benefits need to consider this broad scope.

Who Should Read This Book

You should read this book if you are interested in the architectural, organizational, and cultural changes that are needed to succeed with a microservice architecture. We primarily wrote this book for technology leaders and software architects who want to shift their organizations toward the microservices style of application development. You don't have to be a CTO or enterprise architect to enjoy this book, but we've written our guidance under the assumption that you are able to influence the organizational design, technology platform, and software architecture at your company.

What's In This Book

This book promotes a goal-oriented, design-based approach to microservice architecture. We offer this design-centric approach because, as we talked to several companies about their programs, we discovered one of the keys to their success was the willingness to *not* stick to a single tool or process as they attempted to increase their company's time-to-market while maintaining—even increasing—their systems' safety and resilience.

The companies we talked to offered a wide range of services including live video and audio streaming service, foundation-level virtual services in the cloud, and support for classic brick-and-mortar operations. While these companies' products vary, we learned that the principles of speed and safety "at scale" were a common thread. They each worked to provide the same system properties in their own unique ways—ways that fit the key business values and goals of the company.

It's the properties and values that we focus on in this book, and the patterns and practices we see companies employ in order to reach their unique goals. If you're looking for a way to identify business goals for your microservices adoption, practical guidance on how to design individual microservices and the system they form, and tips on how to overcome common architectural challenges, this is your book!

The Outline

The book is organized into three parts. The first part (Chapters 1–2) identifies the principles and practices of microservice architecture and the benefits they can provide. This section will be valuable to anyone who needs to justify the use of microservices within their organization and provide some background on how other organizations have started on this journey.

The second part (Chapters 3–4) introduces a design-based approach to microservice architecture, identifies a series of common processes and practices we see repeated through successful microservice systems, and provides some implementation guidance on executing the various elements for your company's microservice implementation.

The third and final part (Chapters 5–7) provides a set of practical recipes and practices to help companies identify ways to introduce and support microservices, meet immediate challenges, and plan for and respond to the inevitably changing business environment ahead.

Here's a quick rundown of the chapters:

Chapter 1, The Microservices Way
> This chapter outlines the principles, practices, and culture that define microservice architecture.

Chapter 2, The Microservices Value Proposition
> This chapter examines the benefits of microservice architecture and some techniques to achieve them.

Chapter 3, Designing Microservice Systems
> This chapter explores the system aspects of microservices and illustrates a design process for microservice architecture.

Chapter 4, Establishing a Foundation
> This chapter discusses the core principles for microservice architecture, as well as the platform components and cultural elements needed to thrive.

Chapter 5, Service Design
> This chapter takes the "micro" design view, examining the fundamental design concepts for individual microservices.

Chapter 6, System Design and Operations
> This chapter takes the "macro" design view, analyzing the critical design areas for the software system made up of the collection of microservices.

Chapter 7, Adopting Microservices in Practice
> This chapter provides practical guidance on how to deal with common challenges organizations encounter as they introduce microservice architecture.

Chapter 8, Epilogue
> Finally, this chapter examines microservices and microservice architecture in a timeless context, and emphasizes the central theme of the book: adaptability to change.

What's Not In This Book

The aim of this book is to arm readers with practical information and a way of thinking about microservices that is timeless and effective. This is not a coding book. There is a growing body of code samples and open source projects related to microservices available on the Web, notably on GitHub (*https://github.com/*) and on sites like InfoQ (*http://www.infoq.com/*). In addition, the scope of this domain is big and we can only go so deep on the topics we cover. For more background on the concepts we discuss, check out our reading list in Appendix A.

While we provide lots of guidance and advice—advice based on our discussions with a number of companies designing and implementing systems using microservice architecture patterns—we do not tell readers which product to buy, which open source project to adopt, or how to design and test component APIs. Instead, we offer insight into the thinking processes and practices of experienced and successful companies actually *doing* the work of microservices. If you're looking for simple answers, you're likely to be disappointed in some of the material here. If, on the other hand, you're looking for examples of successful microservice companies and the kinds of principles, practices, and processes they employ, this book is for you.

Conventions Used in This Book

The following typographical conventions are used in this book:

Italic
> Indicates new terms, URLs, email addresses, filenames, and file extensions.

Constant width

Used for program listings, as well as within paragraphs to refer to program elements such as variable or function names, databases, data types, environment variables, statements, and keywords.

Constant width bold

Shows commands or other text that should be typed literally by the user.

Constant width italic

Shows text that should be replaced with user-supplied values or by values determined by context.

 This element signifies a tip or suggestion.

 This element signifies a general note.

 This element indicates a warning or caution.

Safari® Books Online

 *Safari Books Online* is an on-demand digital library that delivers expert content in both book and video form from the world's leading authors in technology and business.

Technology professionals, software developers, web designers, and business and creative professionals use Safari Books Online as their primary resource for research, problem solving, learning, and certification training.

Safari Books Online offers a range of plans and pricing for enterprise, government, education, and individuals.

Members have access to thousands of books, training videos, and prepublication manuscripts in one fully searchable database from publishers like O'Reilly Media,

Prentice Hall Professional, Addison-Wesley Professional, Microsoft Press, Sams, Que, Peachpit Press, Focal Press, Cisco Press, John Wiley & Sons, Syngress, Morgan Kaufmann, IBM Redbooks, Packt, Adobe Press, FT Press, Apress, Manning, New Riders, McGraw-Hill, Jones & Bartlett, Course Technology, and hundreds more. For more information about Safari Books Online, please visit us online.

How to Contact Us

Please address comments and questions concerning this book to the publisher:

O'Reilly Media, Inc.
1005 Gravenstein Highway North
Sebastopol, CA 95472
800-998-9938 (in the United States or Canada)
707-829-0515 (international or local)
707-829-0104 (fax)

To comment or ask technical questions about this book, send email to *bookquestions@oreilly.com*.

For more information about our books, courses, conferences, and news, see our website at *http://www.oreilly.com*.

Find us on Facebook: *http://facebook.com/oreilly*

Follow us on Twitter: *http://twitter.com/oreillymedia*

Watch us on YouTube: *http://www.youtube.com/oreillymedia*

Acknowledgments

The authors would like to thank Brian MacDonald, Holger Reinhardt, Ian Kelly, and Brian Mitchell for helping to clarify, focus, and structure the content of the book. We would also like to thank John Allspaw, Stu Charlton, Adrian Cockcroft, Mel Conway, James Lewis, Ruth Malan, and Jon Moore for helping to guide our thinking along the way.

A number of early microservice adopters provided insight for the book. We would like to thank Greg Bell, Ken Britton, Beier Cai, Steve Cullingworth, Bill Monkman, Mike Sample, and Jeremy Skelton of Hootsuite; Chris Munns of Amazon; Clay Garrard and Patrick Devlin of Disney; and Christian Deger of AutoScout24.

The book would not have been completed without the support of CA Technologies. We would like to thank Alex Jones, Jeff Miller, Ryan Blain, Jaime Ryan, Sam Macklin, and many others for their help. We would also like to thank Leia Poritz, Heather

Scherer, Rachel Roumeliotis, Sharon Cordesse, Kristen Brown, Christina Edwards, and the team at O'Reilly Media.

Finally and most importantly, the authors would like to thank their families. Mike thanks Lee, Shannon, Jesse, and Dana for putting up with his usual travel and writing shenanigans. Matt thanks Chris, Daniel, and Josiah for their love and support. Ronnie thanks his father for putting him in front of a computer. Irakli thanks Ana, Dachi, Maia, Diana, and Malkhaz for their unconditional support and encouragement.

PART I

Understanding Microservices

Balancing Speed and Safety

If you drive around Sweden you'll see variations of the same road markings, road signs, and traffic signals that are used everywhere else in the developed world. But Sweden is a remarkably safer place for road users than the rest of the world. In fact, in 2013 it was among the safest countries in road traffic deaths per 100,000 people (*http://api.co/1qXwA6Q*).

So, how did the Swedes do it? Are they better drivers? Are the traffic laws in Sweden stricter than other countries? Are their roads just better designed? It turns out that the recipe for traffic safety is a combination of all of these things, delivered by an innovative program called Vision Zero.

Vision Zero has a laudable goal—reducing all road accident–related deaths to zero. It aims to achieve this by designing road systems that prioritize safety above all other factors, while still recognizing the importance of keeping traffic moving. In other words, a road system that is designed first and foremost with safety in mind.

At its core, Vision Zero is about culture change. Policymakers, traffic system designers, and citizens have a shared belief that the safety of pedestrians and drivers is more valuable than the need to move from place to place as quickly as possible. This culture of safety drives individual behavior, which can result in a more desirable outcome for the traffic system.

In addition, the road system itself is designed to be safer. Traffic designers apply speed limits, road signs, and traffic movement patterns in a way that benefits the overall safety of the system. For example, while it is necessary to ensure the movement of cars on the road, speed is limited to a level that the human body could withstand in a collision given the technical standards of the vehicles and roads that exist. While speed limits may impact drivers' ability to get to their destination as quickly as possible, the design decision is always driven by the requirement to protect human life. Where most road systems are designed to facilitate movement (or speed) in a safe way, Vision Zero systems incorporate movement into a system primarily designed for safety.

The road designers are continuously making trade-offs that favor the safety of its users. Instead of solely relying on skilled drivers who know how to avoid common mistakes, Vision Zero designers create roads that account for the errors and miscalculations that many human drivers inevitably make. While it is the driver's responsibility to adhere to the rules of the road, the system designers must do their best to protect humans even in situations where drivers do not conform.

All in all, the Vision Zero approach seems to work. While they haven't reduced fatalities to zero yet, the program has been so successful in improving safety within Sweden that other cities like New York and Seattle are adopting it and hoping to see similar results in their own traffic systems. In the end, this success was made possible by combining improvements to policy, technology, and infrastructure in a holistic manner. Vision Zero adopts a systematic approach to design in a safety-first manner.

Just like traffic systems, software systems become more complex as their scale—in the form of scope, volume, and user interactions—increases. And like road designers, software architects and engineers must maintain a balance of speed and safety in their software systems. Software development organizations have used microservice architecture to achieve faster delivery and greater safety as the scale of their systems increase. The holistic, consciously designed approach of Vision Zero suggests an approach to microservice architecture that organizations can take to achieve the balance of speed and safety that meets their goals.

CHAPTER 1

The Microservices Way

> Microservices are a thing these days.
>
> —Phil Calçado, former Director of Engineering, SoundCloud

Building solutions with speed and safety at scale.

If you're like most software developers, team leaders, and architects responsible for getting working code out the door of your company, this phrase describes your job in a nutshell. Most of you have probably struggled at this, too. Getting to market quickly seems to imply giving up a bit of safety. Or, conversely, making sure the system is safe, reliable, and resilient means slowing down the pace of feature and bug-fix releases. And "at scale" is just a dream.

However, a few years ago people started talking about companies that were doing just that. Shortening their time-to-market on new releases, actually *improving* their system reliability, and doing it all in runtime environments that were able to respond smoothly to unexpected spikes in traffic. These companies were "doing microservices."

In this chapter we'll explore what microservices are and what it means to build an application the microservices way. To begin with, we'll explore the meaning of the term *microservices* by learning about its origin. Next, we'll take a look at some of the biggest perceived barriers to adopting microservices. Finally, we share a simple perspective on application development that will help you better understand how all the pieces of microservices systems fit together, a balancing act of speed and safety that we call the *microservices way*.

Understanding Microservices

To better understand what microservices are, we need to look at where they came from. We aren't going to recount the entire history of microservices and software architecture, but it's worth briefly examining how microservices came to be. While the term microservices has probably been used in various forms for many years, the association it now has with a particular way of building software came from a meeting attended by a handful of software architects. This group saw some commonality in the way a particular set of companies was building software and gave it a name.

As James Lewis, who was in attendance, remembers it:

> At the end of our three-day meeting, one of us called out a theme—that year it had been clear that many of the problems people were facing in the wild were related to building systems that were too big. "How can I rebuild a part of this," "best ways to implement Strangler," etc.
>
> Turning that on its head, the problem became "how can we build systems that are *replaceable* over being *maintainable*?" We used the term micro apps, I seem to remember.
>
> —James Lewis

James' recollection of the microservices origin story is important not only for historical record, but also because it identifies three concepts that are principal to the style:

Microservices are ideal for **big systems**
The common theme among the problems that people were facing was related to size. This is significant because it highlights a particular characteristic of the microservices style—it is designed to solve problems for systems that are big. But size is a relative measure, and it is difficult to quantify the difference between small, normal, and big. You could of course come up with some way of deciding what constitutes big versus small, perhaps using averages or heuristic measurements, but that would miss the point. What the architects at this gathering were concerned with was not a question of the size of the system. Instead, they were grappling with a situation in which the system was *too* big. What they identified is that systems that grow in size beyond the boundaries we initially define pose particular problems when it comes to changing them. In other words, new problems arise due to their *scale*.

Microservice architecture is **goal-oriented**
Something else we can derive from James' recollection of the day is the focus on a *goal* rather than just a solution. Microservice architecture isn't about identifying a specific collection of practices, rather it's an acknowledgment that software professionals are trying to solve a similar goal using a particular approach. There may be a set of common characteristics that arise from this style of software

development, but the focus is meant to be on solving the initial problem of systems that are too big.

*Microservices are focused on **replaceability***

The revelation that microservices are really about replaceability is the most enlightening aspect of the story. This idea that driving toward replacement of components rather than maintaining existing components get to the very heart of what makes the microservices approach special.

 If you are interested in learning more on the history of microservices, visit *http://api.co/msabook.*

Overwhelmingly, the companies that we talked to have adopted the microservices architectural style as a way of working with systems in which scale is a factor. They are more interested in the goal of improving changeability than finding a universal pattern or process. Finally, the methods that have helped them improve changeability the most are primarily rooted in improving the replaceability of components. These are all characteristics that align well with the core of the microservices ideal.

Adopting Microservices

If you are responsible for implementing technology at your company, the microservices proposition should sound enticing. Chances are you face increasing pressure to improve the changeability of the software you write in order to align better with a business team that wants to be more innovative. It isn't easy to make a system more amenable to change, but the microservice focus on building replaceable components offers some hope.

However, when we've talked to people interested in adopting microservice-style architectures they often have some reservations. Behind the enthusiasm for a new way of approaching their problem is a set of looming uncertainties about the potential damage that this approach might cause to their systems. In particular, after learning more about microservices methods, potential adopters frequently identify the following issues:

1. They have already built a microservice architecture, but they didn't know it had a name.

2. The management, coordination, and control of a microservices system would be too difficult.

3. The microservices style doesn't account for their unique context, environment, and requirements.

While we don't believe that microservices is the answer to every question about a potential architecture choice, we do feel that these particular fears should be better understood before dismissing an opportunity to improve a system. Let's take a look at each of these barriers to adoption in more detail.

"What are microservices? Don't I already have them?"

Earlier in this chapter we shared the story of how microservices got their name, but we never actually came up with a concrete definition. While there is not one single definition for the term "microservice," there are two that we think are very helpful:

> Microservices are small, autonomous services that work together.
>
> —Sam Newman, Thoughtworks

> Loosely coupled service-oriented architecture with bounded contexts.
>
> —Adrian Cockcroft, Battery Ventures

They both emphasize some level of independence, limited scope, and interoperability. We also think that it is important to view "a microservice" in the scope of an existing *system*. For that reason our definition of microservices also includes the architectural element:

> A *microservice* is an independently deployable component of bounded scope that supports interoperability through message-based communication. *Microservice architecture* is a style of engineering highly automated, evolvable software systems made up of capability-aligned microservices.

You may find much of what is described in the preceding definition familiar. In fact, your organization is probably doing something like this already. If you've implemented a service-oriented architecture (SOA), you've already embraced the concept of modularity and message-based communication. If you've implemented DevOps practices you've already invested in automated deployment. If you are an Agile shop, you've already started shaping your culture in a way that fits the microservices advice.

But given that there is no single, authoritative definition, when do you get to proclaim that your architecture is a *microservice architecture*? What is the measure and who gets to decide? Is there such a thing as a "minimum viable microservice architecture"?

The short answer is we don't know. More importantly, we don't care! We've found that the companies that do well with microservices don't dwell on the meaning of this single word. That doesn't mean that definitions are trivial—instead, it's an admission that finding a *universal* meaning for the microservices style is not important when it comes to meeting business goals. Your time is better spent improving your architecture in a way that helps you unlock more business value. For most organizations this means building applications with more resilience and changeability than ever before. What you call that style of application is entirely up to you.

If you are considering adopting a microservice architecture for your organization, consider how effective the existing architecture is in terms of changeability and more specifically replaceability. Are their opportunities to improve? Could you go beyond modularity, Agile practices, or DevOps to gain value? We think you'll stand a better chance at providing value to your business team if you are open to making changes that will get you closer to those goals. Later in this chapter we'll introduce two goals that we believe give you the best chance at success.

"How could this work here?"

Earlier in this chapter we shared perspectives on microservices from Newman, Cock-croft, Lewis, and Fowler. From these comments, it is clear that microservice applications share some important characteristics:

- Small in size
- Messaging enabled
- Bounded by contexts
- Autonomously developed
- Independently deployable
- Decentralized
- Built and released with automated processes

That's a big scope! So big that some people believe that microservices describe a software development utopia—a set of principles so idealistic that they simply can't be realized in the real world. But this type of claim is countered with the growing list of companies who are sharing their microservice success stories with the world. You've probably heard some of those stories already—Netflix, SoundCloud, and Spotify have all gone public about their microservices experiences.

But if you are responsible for the technology division of a bank, hospital, or hotel chain, you might claim that none of these companies look like yours. The microservices stories we hear the most about are from companies that provide streamed content. While this is a domain with incredible pressure to remain resilient and perform at great scale, the business impact of an individual stream failing is simply incomparable to a hotel losing a reservation, a single dollar being misplaced, or a mistake in a medical report.

Does all of this mean that microservices is not a good fit for hotels, banks, and hospitals? We don't think so and neither do the architects we've spoken to from each of those industries. But we have found that the particular way your organization needs to implement a microservice system is likely to differ from the way that Netflix implements theirs. The trick is in having a clear goal and understanding where the dials are to move your organization toward it. Later in this book we'll shed some light on the principles and practices that help microservices companies succeed.

"How would we deal with all the parts? Who is in charge?"

Two microservices characteristics that you might find especially concerning are decentralization and autonomy. Decentralization means that the bulk of the work done within your system will no longer be managed and controlled by a central body. Embracing team autonomy means trusting your development teams to make their own decisions about the software they produce. The key benefit to both of these approaches is that software changes become both easier and faster—less centralization results in fewer bottlenecks and less resistance to change, while more autonomy means decisions can be made much quicker.

But if your organization hasn't worked this way in the past, how confident are you that it could do so in the future? For example, your company probably does its best to prevent the damage that any single person's decisions can have on the organization as a whole. In large companies, the desire to limit negative impact is almost always implemented with centralized controls—security teams, enterprise architecture teams, and the enterprise service bus are all manifestations of this concept. So, how do you reconcile the ideals of a microservice architecture within a risk-averse culture? How do we *govern* the work done by microservices teams?

Similarly, how do you manage the output of all these teams? Who decides which services should be created? How will services communicate efficiently? How will you understand what is happening?

We've found that decentralization and control are not opposing forces. In other words, the idea that there is a trade-off between a decentralized system and a governed system is a myth. But this doesn't mean that you gain the benefits of decentralization and autonomy for free. When you build software in this way, the cost of controlling and managing output increases significantly. In a microservice architecture, the services tend to get simpler, but the architecture tends to get more complex. That complexity is often managed with tooling, automation, and process.

Ultimately, you must come to terms with the fact that asserting control and management of a microservice system is more expensive than in other architectural styles. For many organizations, this cost is justified by a desire for increased system changeability. However, if you believe that the return doesn't adequately outweigh the benefit, chances are this is not the best way to build software in your organization.

The Microservices Way

When you first begin learning about microservice architecture it's easy to get caught up in the tangible parts of the solution. You don't have to look hard to find people who are excited about Docker, continuous delivery, or service discovery. All of these things can help you to build a system that sounds like the microservice systems we've been discussing. But microservices can't be achieved by focusing on a particular set of patterns, process, or tools. Instead, you'll need to stay focused on the goal itself—a system that can make change easier.

More specifically, the real value of microservices is realized when we focus on two key aspects—*speed* and *safety*. Every single decision you make about your software development ends up as a trade-off that impacts these two ideals. Finding an effective balance between them at *scale* is what we call the *microservices way*.

> Speed and Safety at Scale and in Harmony.
>
> —The Microservices Way

The Speed of Change

The desire for speed is a desire for immediate change and ultimately a desire for adaptability. On one hand, we could build software that is capable of changing itself—this might require a massive technological leap and incredibly complex system. But the solution that is more realistic for our present state of technological advancement is to shorten the time it takes for changes to move from individual workers to a production environment.

Years ago, most of us released software in the same way that NASA launches rockets. After deliberate effort and careful quality control, our software was burned into a permanent state and *delivered* to users on tapes, CDs, DVDs, and diskettes. Of course, the popularity of the Web changed the nature of software delivery and the mechanics of releases have become much cheaper and easier. Ease of access combined with improved automation has drastically reduced the cost of a software change. Most organizations have the platforms, tools, and infrastructure in place to implement thousands of application releases within a single day. But they don't. In fact, most teams are happy if they can manage a release in a week. Why is that? The answer of course is that the real deterrent to release speed is the fragility of the software they've produced.

The Safety of Change

Speed of change gets a lot of attention in stories about microservice architecture, but the unspoken, yet equally important counterpart is change safety. After all, "speed kills" and in most software shops nobody wants to be responsible for breaking production. Every change is potentially a breaking change and a system optimized purely for speed is only realistic if the cost of breaking the system is near zero. Most development environments are optimized for release speed, enabling the software developer to make multiple changes in as short a time as possible. On the other hand, most production environments are optimized for safety, restricting the rate of change to those releases that carry the minimum risk of damage.

At Scale

On top of everything else, today's software architect needs to be able to "think big" when building applications. As we heard earlier in this chapter, the microservices style is rooted in the idea of solving the problems that arise when software gets too big. To build at scale means to build software that can continue to work when demand grows beyond our initial expectations. Systems that can work at scale don't break when under pressure; instead they incorporate built-in mechanisms to increase capacity in a safe way. This added dimension requires a special perspective to building software and is essential to the microservices way.

In Harmony

Your life is filled with decisions that impact speed and safety. Not just in the software domain, but in most of your everyday life; how fast are you willing to drive a car to get where you need to be on time? How does that maximum speed change when there is someone else in the car with you? Is that number different if one of your passengers is a child? The need to balance these ideals is something you were probably taught at a young age and you are probably familiar with the well-worn proverb, "haste makes waste."

We've found that all of the characteristics that we associate with microservice architecture (i.e., replaceability, decentralization, context-bound, message-based communication, modularity, etc.) have been employed by practitioners in pursuit of providing speed and safety at scale. This is the reason a universal characteristic-driven definition of microservices is unimportant—the real lessons are found in the practices successful companies have employed in pursuit of this balancing act.

We don't want to give you the wrong idea—microservice architecture is not *limited* to a simple series of decisions regarding speed and safety of change. The microservices domain is actually fairly complex and will require you to understand a wide breadth of concepts that have a great depth of impact. If it was any other way, this would be a very short book.

Instead, we introduce the microservices way in order to help you understand the *essence* of the microservices style. All of the significant properties and patterns that are commonly adopted for this style of architecture reflect attempts to deal with the interplay between these forces. The companies that do this best are the ones that find ways to allow both safety and speed of change to coexist. Organizations that succeed with microservice architecture are able to maintain their system stability while increasing their change velocity. In other words, they created a *harmony* of speed and safety that works for their own context.

The pursuit of this harmony should shape the adoption decisions you make for your own system. Throughout this book we will introduce principles and patterns that have helped companies provide great value to their business. It will be tempting to simply replicate the patterns in your own organizations in exactly the same way. But do your best to first pay attention to the impact of these types of changes on your own organization's harmony. We will do our best to provide you with enough information to connect those dots.

It also means that you may not find your balance in the same way as other companies. We don't expect your organization to work the same as the ones we've highlighted in this book and we don't expect your microservices implementation to be the same either. Instead, we hope that focusing on *the way* that microservices applications are built will help you identify the parts that could work for you.

Summary

In this chapter we introduced the original intent of the microservice architecture concept—to replace complex monolithic applications with software systems made of replaceable components. We also introduced some of the concerns that first-time implementers often have, along with some of the practical realities. Finally, we introduced the microservices way, a goal-driven approach to building adaptable, reliable software. The balance of speed and safety at scale is key to understanding the essence of microservices and will come up again throughout this book. In the next chapter we'll take a closer look at the goals of speed and safety in the context of actual microservice implementations.

CHAPTER 2

The Microservices Value Proposition

The microservice architectural style was defined based on common patterns observed across a number of pioneering organizations. These organizations did not consciously implement a microservice architecture. They evolved to it in pursuit of specific goals.

In this chapter, we will explore the common benefits of microservice architecture and how they drive the higher-order goals from Chapter 1—speed, safety, and scale; illustrate how the goals of microservice architecture deliver business value; define a maturity model for microservice architecture benefits and goals; and finally, apply this information using a goal-oriented approach to microservice architecture.

To start with, let's survey the motivations of some early microservice adopters.

Microservice Architecture Benefits

Why are organizations adopting microservices? What are the motivations and challenges? How can the leaders of these organizations tell that taking on the challenges of managing a collection of small, loosely coupled, independently deployable services is actually paying off for the company? What is the measure of success? Surveying the early adopters of microservices, we find that the answers to these questions vary quite a bit. However, some common themes emerge and tie back to the mantra of "balancing speed and safety at scale."

Werner Vogels of Amazon describes the advantages of their architecture as follows (*http://api.co/24gZrjw*):

> We can scale our operation independently, maintain unparalleled system availability, and introduce new services quickly without the need for massive reconfiguration.
>
> —Werner Vogels, Chief Technology Officer, Amazon Web Services

By focusing on scalability and component independence, Amazon has been able to increase their speed of delivery while also improving the safety—in the form of scalability and availability—of their environment.

UK e-retailer Gilt is another early adopter of microservice architecture. Their Senior Vice President of Engineering, Adrian Trenaman, listed these resulting benefits in an InfoQ article (*http://api.co/gilt-microservices*):

- Lessens dependencies between teams, resulting in faster code to production
- Allows lots of initiatives to run in parallel
- Supports multiple technologies/languages/frameworks
- Enables graceful degradation of service
- Promotes ease of innovation through *disposable code*—it is easy to fail and move on

The first three points help speed up software development, through organizational alignment and independent deployability, as well as polyglotism. The last two points speak to a safe environment that facilitates replaceability of services.

Social media pioneer Hootsuite has observed efficiency benefits in their microservice adoption based on the tunability of the system:

> Some services require high availability, but are low volume, and it's the opposite for other services. A microservice approach allows us to tune for both of these situations, whereas in a monolith it's all or nothing.
>
> —Beier Cai, Director of Software Development, Hootsuite

With a more granular set of components, Hootsuite is able to independently manage their services and achieve greater efficiency.

Clay Garrard, Senior Manager of Cloud Services at Disney, found that although there was work done to modularize the code base of their monolithic applications, the domain boundaries were not clear. This meant that small changes often led to large deployments.

> With microservices, we have reduced the time it takes to deploy a useful piece of code and also reduced the frequency of deploying code that hasn't changed. Ultimately we strive to be flexible in our interpretation of microservice architecture, using its strengths where we can, but realizing that the business does not care about how we achieve results, only that we move quickly with good quality and flexible design.
>
> —Clay Garrard, Senior Manager of Cloud Services, Disney

The primary driver here is speed, as requested directly from the business. However, there is also an emphasis on safety—through independent deployability and testability—as well as future-proofing through composability.

Lastly, SoundCloud sought to solve the following problem when they evolved to a microservice architecture (*http://api.co/1PcIYvk*):

> The monolithic code base we had was so massive and so broad no one knew all of it. People had developed their own areas of expertise and custodianship around submodules of the application.
>
> —Phil Calçado, former Director of Engineering, SoundCloud

By embracing microservices, they were able to overcome this issue and improve the comprehensibility of their software system.

There are common goals and benefits that emerge from these implementation stories. The goal of improving software delivery speed as functional scope grows is realized through greater agility, higher composability, improved comprehensibility, independent service deployability, organizational alignment, and polyglotism. The goal of maintaining software system safety as scale increases is achieved through higher availability and resiliency, better efficiency, independent manageability and replaceability of components, increased runtime scalability, and more simplified testability. Now let's explore how these goals and benefits derive business value for organizations that employ microservice architecture.

Deriving Business Value

Successful companies do not focus on increasing software delivery speed for its own sake. They do it because they are compelled by the speed of their business. Similarly, the level of safety implemented in an organization's software system should be tied to specific business objectives. Conversely, the safety measures must not get in the way of the speed unnecessarily. Balance is required.

For each organization, that balance will be a function of its delivery speed, the safety of its systems, and the growth of the organization's functional scope and scale. Each organization will have its own balance. A media company that aims to reach the widest possible audience for its content may place a much higher value on delivery speed than a retail bank whose compliance requirements mandate specific measures around safety. Nonetheless, in an increasingly digital economy, more companies are recognizing that software development needs to become one of their core competencies.

In this new business environment, where disruptive competitors can cross industry boundaries or start up from scratch seemingly overnight, fast software delivery is essential to staying ahead of the competition and achieving sustainable growth. In fact, each of the microservice architecture benefits that drive delivery speed contribute real business value:

- *Agility* allows organizations to deliver new products, functions, and features more quickly and pivot more easily if needed.
- *Composability* reduces development time and provides a compound benefit through reusability over time.
- *Comprehensibility* of the software system simplifies development planning, increases accuracy, and allows new resources to come up to speed more quickly.
- *Independent deployability* of components gets new features into production more quickly and provides more flexible options for piloting and prototyping.
- *Organizational alignment* of services to teams reduces ramp-up time and encourages teams to build more complex products and features iteratively.
- *Polyglotism* permits the use of the right tools for the right task, thus accelerating technology introduction and increasing solution options.

Likewise, digital native consumers expect always-on services and are not shy about changing corporate allegiances. Outages or lost information can cause them to take their business elsewhere. A safe software system is indispensable. The safety-aligned benefits discussed earlier also provide particular business value:

- Greater *efficiency* in the software system reduces infrastructure costs and reduces the risk of capacity-related service outages.
- *Independent manageability* contributes to improved efficiency, and also reduces the need for scheduled downtime.
- *Replaceability* of components reduces the technical debt that can lead to aging, unreliable environments.
- Stronger *resilience* and higher *availability* ensure a good customer experience.
- Better *runtime scalability* allows the software system to grow or shrink with the business.
- Improved *testability* allows the business to mitigate implementation risks.

Clearly, microservice architecture has the potential to provide numerous business benefits. However, not every organization needs every benefit, and not every microservice architecture is capable of delivering all of them. With that in mind, let's now look at how an organization can combine its business objectives with the potential benefits of microservice architecture to tailor a goal-oriented approach.

Defining a Goal-Oriented, Layered Approach

In spite of the fact that microservice architecture was originally a reaction to the limitations of monolithic applications, there is a fair amount of guidance in the industry that says new applications should still be built as monoliths first (*http://martin fowler.com/bliki/MonolithFirst.html*). The thinking is that only through the creation and ownership of a monolith can the right service boundaries be identified. This path is certainly well trodden, given that early microservice adopters generally went through the process of unbundling their own monolithic applications. The "monolith first" approach also appears to follow Gall's Law (*http://amzn.to/27RdQYu*), which states that, "A complex system that works is invariably found to have evolved from a simple system that worked." However, is a monolithic application architecture the only simple system starting point? Is it possible to start simple with a microservice architecture?

In fact, the complexity of a software system is driven by its scale. Scale comes in the form of functional scope, operational magnitude, and change frequency. The first companies to use microservice architecture made the switch from monolithic applications once they passed a certain scale threshold. With the benefit of hindsight, and with an analysis of the common goals and benefits of microservice architecture, we can map out a set of layered characteristics to consider when adopting microservice architecture.

Modularized Microservice Architecture

> Modularity … is to a technological economy what the division of labor is to a manufacturing one.
>
> —W. Brian Arthur, author of *The Nature of Technology*

At its most basic level, microservice architecture is about breaking up an application or system into smaller parts. A software system that is modularized arbitrarily will obviously have some limitations, but there is still a potential upside. Network-accessible modularization facilitates automation and provides a concrete means of abstraction. Beyond that, some of the microservice architecture benefits discussed earlier already apply at this base layer.

To help software delivery speed, modularized services are independently deployable. It is also possible to take a polyglot approach to tool and platform selection for individual services, regardless of what the service boundaries are. With respect to safety, services can be managed individually at this layer. Also, the abstracted service interfaces allow for more granular testing.

This is the most technologically focused microservice architecture layer. In order to address this layer and achieve its associated benefits, you must establish a foundation for your microservice architecture. This will be discussed in detail in Chapter 4.

Cohesive Microservice Architecture

> The greater the cohesion of individual modules in the system, the lower the coupling between modules will be.
>
> —Larry Constantine and Edward Yourdon, authors of *Structured Design: Fundamentals of a Discipline of Computer Program and Systems Design*

The next layer to consider in your microservice architecture is the cohesion of services. In order to have a cohesive microservice architecture, it must already be modularized. Achieving service cohesion comes from defining the right service boundaries and analyzing the semantics of the system. The concept of domains is useful at this layer, whether they are business-oriented or defined by some other axis.

A cohesive microservice architecture can enable software speed by aligning the system's services with the supporting organization's structure. It can also yield composable services that are permitted to change at the pace the business dictates, rather than through unnecessary dependencies. Reducing the dependencies of a system featuring cohesive services also facilitates replaceability of services. Moreover, service cohesion lessens the need for highly orchestrated message exchanges between components, thereby creating a more efficient system.

It takes a synthesized view of business, technology, and organizational considerations to build a cohesive system. This can be addressed through service design, which is the focus of Chapter 5.

Systematized Microservice Architecture

> The key in making great and growable systems is much more to design how its modules communicate rather than what their internal properties and behaviors should be.[1]
>
> —Alan Kay, 1998 email to the Squeak-dev list

The final and most advanced layer to consider in a microservice architecture is its system elements. After breaking the system into pieces through modularization, and addressing the services' contents through cohesion, it is time to examine the interrelationships between the services. This is where the greatest level of complexity in the system needs to be addressed, but also where the biggest and longest-lasting benefits can be realized.

---

1 *http://api.co/kay-systems*

There are two ways speed of delivery is impacted in a systematized microservice architecture. Although a single service may be understandable even in a modularized microservice architecture, the overall software system is only comprehensible when the connectivity between services is known. Also, agility is only possible when the impacts of changes on the whole system can be identified and assessed rapidly. This applies on the safety side as well, where runtime scalability is concerned. Lastly, although individual components may be isolated and made resilient in a modularized or cohesive microservice architecture, the system availability is not assured unless the interdependencies of the components are understood.

Dealing with complex systems requires a careful approach based on influence versus control. The system aspects of microservice architecture are discussed in detail in Chapters 3 and 6.

Maturity Model for Microservice Architecture Goals and Benefits

These layered characteristics—modularized, cohesive, and systematized—help to define a maturity model that serves a number of purposes. First, it classifies the benefits according to phase and goal (speed or safety) as discussed previously. Secondly, it illustrates the relative impact and priority of benefits as scale and complexity increase. Lastly, it shows the activities needed to address each architectural phase. This maturity model is depicted in Figure 2-1.

Note that an organization's microservice architecture can be at different phases for different goals. Many companies have become systematized in their approach to safety—through automation and other operational considerations—without seeking the speed-aligned system-level benefits. The point of this model is not for every organization to achieve systematized actualization with their microservice architecture. Rather, the model is meant to clarify goals and benefits in order to help organizations focus their microservice strategies and prepare for what could come next.

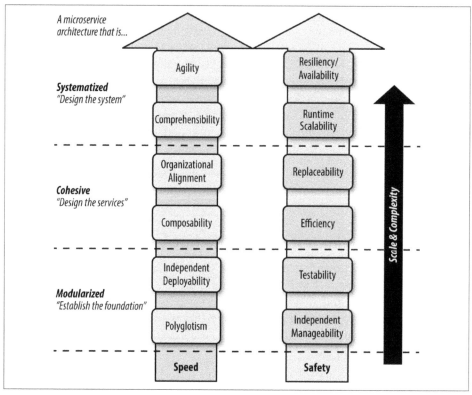

Figure 2-1. A maturity model for microservice architecture goals and benefits

Applying the Goal-Oriented, Layered Approach

Now we have a good understanding of how a microservice architecture can bring value to an organization, and a model for understanding what characteristics can bring what goals and benefits at what stage of adoption. But what about your organization? What are your business goals? What problems do you need to solve? It is a common misstep to start down the microservices path for its own sake without thinking about the specific benefits you are targeting. In other cases, some organizations aim for a high-level goal and then only implement one aspect of microservices while ignoring its founding conditions. For example, an organization with a high-level divide between development and operations—an organizational red flag—might execute a containerization strategy on their existing applications and then wonder why they didn't speed up their software development sufficiently. A broad perspective is needed.

To begin with, define the high-level business objectives you want to accomplish, and then weigh these against the dual goals of speed and safety. Within that context, consider the distinct benefits you are targeting. You can then use the maturity model to determine the complexity of the goal, and identify the best approach to achieve it.

Holger Reinhardt, CTO of the German digital media group Haufe-Lexware, provides an example of a goal-oriented approach in action. One of Haufe's initial attempts at microservice architecture was on their monolithic service platform, which included functions such as user management and license management. The first attempt was explicitly focused on changing the architecture from monolith to service-enabled software system. The results were not positive. However, when they evaluated the main issues with the application—particularly the operational inefficiencies around it —they changed their approach from refactoring the existing architecture to automating the problematic deployment process. Through a small investment, they were able to take their service platform deployment downtime from 5 days to 30 minutes. Their next iteration will focus on reducing QA time through automation and a switch in methodology from white-box to black-box testing. Following these methodological changes, they will identify the domains in their monolithic application that require the greatest speed of innovation and unbundle those first. By taking an iterative approach tied to clear goals, they are able to measure success quickly and change course if needed.

Summary

This chapter has covered a lot of ground that should help you define a strategy for applying a microservice architecture in your organization. We first analyzed the reasons the early adopters of microservice architecture chose this style. Next, we looked into the common goals and benefits of microservices, how they relate to each other, and what business objectives they can drive. Lastly, we defined a maturity model that can be used to target the right goals and benefits for applying a microservice architecture in your organization. You should now be ready to roll up your sleeves and learn a design-based approach to microservice architecture.

PART II

Microservice Design Principles

The Flaw of Averages

In the 1950s, the US Air Force launched a study into the causes of pilot errors and part of that study focused on the physical dimensions of the pilots and their cockpit control systems. The cockpits had been initially designed based on assumed physical averages of pilots and it was assumed that pilots had grown larger over time and that the design needed to be updated.

 This story comes from the book *The End of Average* by Todd Rose (Harper Collins, 2016). Rose has given a TEDx talk on the subject of averages and is a leading proponent of an interdisciplinary field called "The Science of the Individual" (*http://lsi.gse.harvard.edu/home-0*).

It fell to 23-year-old Lt. Gilbert Daniels to lead the painstaking process of carefully measuring over 4,000 pilots on 140 different physcial dimensions and then analyze the results. Along the way, Daniels got the idea to go beyond the initial plan to compute the averages of all 140 dimensions in order to construct what the military deemed the "average pilot." Daniels wanted to know just how many of the 4,000 pilots he had measured actually were *average*—i.e., how many fit the computed values the military was aiming to use to redesign the airplane cockpits?

By taking just ten of the many dimensions he was working with (height, chest size, sleeve length, etc.), Daniels constructed what he defined as the average pilot. Daniels also posited that anyone who fell within a 30% range of the target number for a dimension would be included in his list of average pilots. For example, the average pilot height turned out to be 5'9". So, for Daniels, anyone who measured 5'7" to 5'11" would be counted as average for height. Daniels then proceeded to check each of his 4,000 subjects to discover just how many of them would score within the average for *every* dimension. He was looking for all the pilots who could be considered completely average. To everyone's surprise, the total count was zero. There was not one single pilot that fell within 30% of the average for *all* ten dimensions. As Daniels wrote in his paper *The "Average Man"?* (*http://api.co/average-man*):

> As an abstract representation of a mythical individual most representative of a given population, the *average man* is convenient to grasp in our minds. Unfortunately he doesn't exist.
>
> —Lt. Gilbert Daniels, *The "Average Man"?*

It turns out there *is no such thing as an average pilot*. Designing a cockpit for the average pilot results in a cockpit configuration that fits no one. Intuitively, this makes sense to most of us. While averages are helpful when looking for trends in a group, the resulting "profile" from this group does not exist in real life. Averages help us focus on trends or broad strokes but do not describe any actual existing examples.

The reason for this difference between real pilots and the average pilot can be summed up in what Rose calls *the principle of jaggedness*. When measuring individuals on a multidimensional set of criteria (height, arm length, girth, hand size, and so forth), there are so many varying combinations that no one individual is likely to exhibit the average value for *all* dimensions. And designing for an individual that exhibits *all* those averages will result in a poor fit for every *actual* person.

This principle of jaggedness is important to keep in mind when designing software architecture, too. Designing for an ideal or average is likely to result in a model that fits no single purpose well. Guidance that calls out specific measurements of an *ideal microservice* or *canonical model* for microservices is likely to have traits that fit no existing microservice implementation. Ideals are just that—not realities.

The solution that eventually worked for the US Air Force was to incorporate variability into the design of airplane cockpits. For example, creating an adjustable seat, the ability to modify the tilt and length of the steering column, and moving the foot pedals forward or back are all examples of designing in variability. This works because the *exact dimensions* of any single element in the design are not as important as the ability to identify the important dimensions that need to support variability.

CHAPTER 3

Designing Microservice Systems

So far we've learned that companies building applications in the microservices way do more than just implement small components. We now know that there isn't a strict definition for what constitutes a microservice architecture. Instead, the focus is on building applications that balance speed and safety at scale, primarily through replaceability. Throughout the remaining chapters of this book we will dive deeper into the details of microservice adoption. But considering what you've learned about microservices systems so far, one thing should be clear—there are a *lot* of moving parts to consider. The hallmark of a microservice architecture might be smaller services, but following the microservices way will require you to think *big*. You'll need to tune your culture, organization, architecture, interfaces, and services in just the right way to gain the balance of speed and safety at scale.

In this chapter we will lay the groundwork for thinking about your application in a way that helps you unlock the potential value of a microservices system. The concepts introduced are rooted in some pretty big domains: design, complexity, and systems thinking. But you don't need to be an expert in any of those fields to be a good microservice designer. Instead, we will highlight a model-driven way of thinking about your application that encapsulates the essential parts of complexity and systems thinking. Finally, at the end of this chapter we will introduce an example of a design process that can help promote a design-driven approach to microservices implementation.

The Systems Approach to Microservices

We've found that many first-time adopters of microservices tend to focus on the services that need to be built. But in order to develop applications in the microservices way, you'll need to conceptualize the design as much more than isolated, individual service designs. That doesn't mean that the design of services can be ignored—just like cars and pedestrians are essential to a traffic system, services are the key ingredient of a microservice system. But thinking in services terms alone isn't enough; instead you'll need to consider how all aspects of the system can work together to form an *emergent* behavior. Emergent behaviors are the ones that are greater than the sum of their parts and for a microservices application this includes the runtime behavior that emerges when we connect individual services together and the organizational behavior that gets us there.

 Emergence is an essential part of the science of complexity and is a key indicator of system complexity. Complexity scientist Melanie Mitchell (known for her work at the Santa Fe Institute) often uses ant colonies to illustrate emergence and complexity: predicting the behavior of a single ant is trivial, but predicting the behavior of an entire ant colony is much more difficult.

A microservices system encompasses all of the things about your organization that are related to the application it produces. This means that the structure of your organization, the people who work there, the way they work, and the outputs they produce are all important system factors. Equally important are runtime architectural elements such as service coordination, error handling, and operational practices. In addition to the wide breadth of subject matter that you need to consider, there is the additional challenge that all of these elements are interconnected—a change to one part of the system can have an unforeseen impact on another part. For example, a change to the size of an implementation team can have a profound impact on the work that the implementation team produces.

If you implement the right decisions at the right times you can influence the behavior of the system and produce the behaviors you want. But that is often easier said than done. Grappling with all of these system elements at the same time is difficult. In fact, you might find it especially challenging to conceptualize all of the moving parts of the microservice system in your head. What we are learning is that microservice systems are complex!

Complexity scientists face a similar challenge when they work with complex systems. With all of the interconnected parts and the complex emergence that results, it is very difficult to understand how the parts work together. In particular, it is difficult to predict the results that can arise from a change to the system. So, they do what scientists have always done—they develop a model.

The models mathematicians develop to study complex systems allow them to more accurately understand and predict the behavior of a system. But this is a field in its infancy and the models they produce tend to be very complicated. We don't expect you to understand the mathematics of complexity, nor do we think it will be particularly helpful in creating better microservice applications. But we do believe that a model-based approach can help all of us conceptualize our system of study and will make it easier for us talk about the parts of the system.

With that in mind, Figure 3-1 depicts a microservice design model comprised of five parts: Service, Solution, Process and Tools, Organization, and Culture.

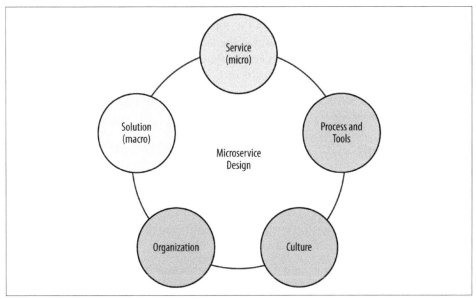

Figure 3-1. The microservice system design model

In truth, each of these design elements are deserving of their own book and we point you to some great sources in the reading list in Appendix A. But the goal of this model is to highlight the major areas of concern and the parts of the system you need to influence in order to succeed with this architectural style.

Service

Implementing well-designed microservices and APIs are essential to a microservice system. In a microservice system, the services form the atomic building blocks from which the entire organism is built. If you can get the design, scope, and granularity of your service just right you'll be able to induce complex behavior from a set of components that are deceptively simple.

In Chapter 5 we'll give you some guidance on designing effective microservices and APIs.

Solution

A solution architecture is distinct from the individual service design elements because it represents a macro view of our solution. When designing a particular microservice your decisions are bounded by the need to produce a single output—the service itself. Conversely, when designing a solution architecture your decisions are bounded by the need to coordinate all the inputs and outputs of multiple services. This macro-level view of the system allows the designer to induce more desirable system behavior. For example, a solution architecture that provides discovery, safety, and routing features can reduce the complexity of individual services.

We will dive into the patterns that you can employ to produce good microservice system behavior in Chapter 6.

Process and Tools

Your microservice system is not just a byproduct of the service components that handle messages at runtime. The system behavior is also a result of the processes and tools that workers in the system use to do their job. In the microservice's system, this usually includes tooling and processes related to software development, code deployment, maintenance, and product management.

Choosing the right processes and tools is an important factor in producing good microservice system behavior. For example, adopting standardized processes like DevOps and Agile or tools like Docker containers can increase the changeability of your system. In Chapters 4 and 6 we will take a closer look at the processes and tools that can have the biggest impact on a microservices system.

Organization

How we work is often a product of who we work with and how we communicate. From a microservice system perspective, organizational design includes the structure, direction of authority, granularity, and composition of teams. Many of the companies that have had success with microservice architecture point to their organizational design as a key ingredient. But organizational design is incredibly context-sensitive and you may find yourself in a terrible situation if you try to model your 500+ employee enterprise structure after a 10-person startup (and vice versa).

A good microservice system designer understands the implications of changing these organizational properties and knows that good service design is a byproduct of good organizational design. We will dive deeper into team design concepts in Chapter 4.

Culture

Of all the microservice system domains, culture is perhaps the most intangible yet may also be the most important. We can broadly define culture as a set of values, beliefs, or ideals that are shared by all of the workers within an organization. Your organization's culture is important because it shapes all of the atomic decisions that people within the system will make. This large scope of influence is what makes it such a powerful tool in your system design endeavor.

Much like organizational design, culture is a context-sensitive feature of your system. What works in Japan may not work in the United States and what works in a large insurance firm may not work at an ecommerce company. So, you'll need to be cautious when attempting to emulate the practices that work in a company whose culture you admire. There is no recipe or playbook that will guarantee you the same results.

As important as it is, the culture of an organization is incredibly difficult to measure. Formal methods of surveying and modeling exist, but many business and technology leaders evaluate the culture of their teams in a more instinctual way. You can get a sense of the culture of your organization through your daily interactions with team members, team products, and the customers they cater to.

However you gauge it, culture is often an indication of the impact of other parts of your system. Shared ideals shape how people do their work and how they work will in turn shape their organizational view. This is the interconnected nature of the system.

Embracing Change

Time is an essential element of a microservice system and failing to account for it is a grave mistake. All of the decisions you make about the organization, culture, processes, services, and solutions should be rooted in the notion that change is inevitable. You cannot afford to be purely deterministic in your system design; instead, you should design adaptability into the system as a feature.

There is good reason for taking this perspective: first, trying to determine what the end state of your organization and solution design should look like is a near impossible task. Second, it is unlikely that the context in which you made your design decisions will stay the same. Changes in requirements, markets, and technology all have a way of making today's good decisions obsolete very quickly.

A good microservice designer understands the need for adaptability and endeavors to continually improve the system instead of working to simply produce a solution. We give you some practical patterns and tools for improving system adaptability in the third part of this book.

Putting it Together: The Holistic System

When put together all of these design elements form the microservices system. They are interconnected and a change to one element can have a meaningful and sometimes unpredictable impact on other elements. The system changes over time and is unpredictable. It produces behavior that is greater than the behavior of its individual components. It adapts to changing contexts, environments, and stimuli.

In short, the microservices system is complex and teasing desirable behaviors and outcomes from that system isn't an easy task. But some organizations have had enormous success in doing so and we can learn from their examples.

Standardization and Coordination

> To be precise, one cannot speak of leaders who cause organizations to achieve superlative performance, for no one can cause it to happen. Leaders can only recognize and modify conditions which prevent it.
>
> —Dee Hock, author of *The Art of Chaordic Leadership*

Almost all of us work in organizations that operate within constraints. These constraints arise because the wrong type of system behavior can be harmful to the organization, even resulting in the organization failing as a result of particularly bad behavior. For example, a banking technology system that makes it easy to steal someone else's money or a tax system that fails to protect its users' private information are unacceptable.

With the cost of unwanted system behavior so high, it's no wonder that so many architects and designers do their best to control system behavior. In practice, the system designer decides that there is some behavior or expectation that must be universally applied to the actors within the system. Policies, governance, and audits are all introduced as a way of policing the behavior of the system and ensuring that the actors conform. In other words, some parts of the system are standardized.

But true control of this type of complex system is an illusion. You have as much chance of guaranteeing that your banking system will be perfectly secure as a farmer does of guaranteeing that his crops will always grow. No matter how many rules, checks, and governance methods you apply you are always at the mercy of actors in a system that can make poor decisions.

Instead, all of these mechanisms of control act as system influencers that greatly increase the likelihood of the results you want. Mastering the system you are designing and making it do the things you want requires you to develop the right standards, make sure the standards are being applied, and measure the results of the changes you are making.

However, control of the system comes at a steep price. Standardization is the enemy of adaptability and if you standardize too many parts of your system you risk creating something that is costly and difficult to change.

In his book *Structure in Fives*, organizational designer Henry Mintzberg identifies some of the coordination mechanisms and standards that make the biggest differences for organizational systems. In particular, he identifies standardization of work outputs, worker skills, and work processes as having the most impact.

> Don't be scared off by our use of the word "standardization"! When we talk about standards, we mean the established norms and accepted ways of working that exist within an organization. The goal of this section is to understand the system impact when standardization is focused on different parts of the company.

Standardizing process

We've already talked about how processes and tools are important for the behavior that emerges from our system. By standardizing the way that people work and the tools they use, you can influence the behavior in a more predictable way. For example, standardizing a deployment process that reduces the time for component deployment may improve the overall changeability of the system as the cost of new deployments decreases.

Standardizing how we work has broad-reaching implications on the type of work we can produce, the kind of people we hire, and the culture of an organization. The Agile methodology is a great example of process standardization. Agile institutionalizes the concept that change should be introduced in small measurable increments that allow the organization to handle change easier. One observable system impact for Agile teams is that the output they produce begins to change. Software releases become smaller and measurability becomes a feature of the product they output. There are also usually follow-on effects to culture and organizational design.

In addition to process standardization, most companies employ some form of tool standardization as well. In fact, many large organizations have departments whose sole purpose is to define the types of tools their workers are allowed to utilize. For example, some firms forbid the use of open source software and limit their teams to the use of centrally approved software, procured by a specialist team.

The microservices tooling space is moving very quickly and we are certain that any discussion of particular microservice tools would be out of date by the time this book is published. But we make an effort to describe the type of tools that are particularly important to standardize in Chapter 4, along with some examples of tools that are particularly relevant at the moment.

Standardizing outputs

We can define a team as a group of workers who take a set of inputs and transform them into one or more outputs. Output standardization is way of setting a universal standard for what that output should look like. For example, in an assembly line the output of the line workers is standardized—everyone on the line must produce exactly the same result. Any deviation from the standard output is considered a failure.

In a microservices system, a team takes a set of requirements and turns those into a microservice. So, the service is the output and the face of that output is the interface (or API) that provides access to the features and data the microservice provides. In fact, from the microservice consumer perspective, the API *is* the output, as they have no visibility of the implementation behind it.

In the microservices context, output standardization often means developing some standards for the APIs that expose the services. For example, you might decide that all the organization's services should have an HTTP interface or that all services should be capable of subscribing to and emitting events. Some organizations even standardize how the interfaces should be designed in an effort to improve the usability, changeability, and overall experience of using the service. In Chapter 5 we will dive deeper into the types of API standardization that make sense for microservice systems and the benefits and costs of different types of interface styles.

Standardizing people

You can also decide to standardize the types of people that do the work within your organization. For example, you could introduce a minimum skill requirement for anyone who wants to work on a microservice team. In fact, many of the companies that have shared microservice stories point to the skill level of their people as a primary characteristic of their success.

Standardizing skills or talent can be an effective way of introducing more autonomy into your microservices system. When the people who are implementing the services are more skilled they have a better chance of making decisions that will create the system behavior you want.

All organizations have some level of minimum skill and experience level for their workers, but organizations that prioritize skill standardization often set very high specialist requirements in order to reap system benefits. If only the best and brightest are good enough to work within your system, be prepared to pay a high cost to maintain that standard.

Standardization trade-offs

Standardizing helps you exert influence over your system, but you don't have to choose just one of these standards to utilize. But keep in mind that while they aren't mutually exclusive, the introduction of different modes of standardization can create unintended consequences in other parts of the system.

For example, you might decide to standardize on the APIs that all microservices expose because you want to reduce the cost of connecting things together in your solution architecture. To do this you might prescribe a set of rules for the types of APIs that developers are allowed to create and institute a review process to police this standardization. As an example, many organizations standardize a way of documenting the interfaces that are created. At the moment Swagger (also called OpenAPI) is a popular example of an interface description language, but there are many others (WADL, Blueprint, RAML, etc.).

But we may find that constraining the types of APIs our people are allowed to produce limits the types of tools they can use to create them. It might be the case that the development tool we want everyone to use doesn't support the interface description language we have already chosen. In other words, the decision to standardize the team's output has had unintended consequences on the team's work process. This happens because standardization is an attempt to remove uncertainty from our system, but comes at the cost of reducing innovation and changeability.

The benefit of standardization is a reduction in the set of all possible outcomes. It gives us a way to shape the system by setting constraints and boundaries for the actions that people within the system can take. But this benefit comes at a cost. Standardization also constrains the autonomy of individual decision-makers.

The challenge for designers is to introduce just enough standardization to achieve the best emergent system outcome, while also employing standards and constraints that complement each other. Throughout this book we will highlight standardization techniques that will be useful for you in your microservices system, along with the possible repercussions of using them.

A Microservices Design Process

> The very first step of a service design process is to design the process itself.
>
> —Marc Stickdorn, author of *This is Service Design Thinking*

Professional designers know that the secret to great design is using the right design process. Where others apply expert advice or make false assumptions about the impact of their design decisions, a good designer employs a process that helps them continually get closer to the best product. This doesn't mean that you never have to make assumptions or that expert guidance is necessarily wrong. Instead, it means that your best chance at designing the microservice system you want is to work with a process that helps you understand the impact of your assumptions and the applicability of advice as you change the system.

Figure 3-2 illustrates a framework for a design process that you can use in your own microservice system designs. In practice, it is likely that you'll need to customize the process to fit within your own unique constraints and context. You might end up using these design activities in a different order than given here. You may also decide that some activities aren't applicable to your goals or that other steps need to be added.

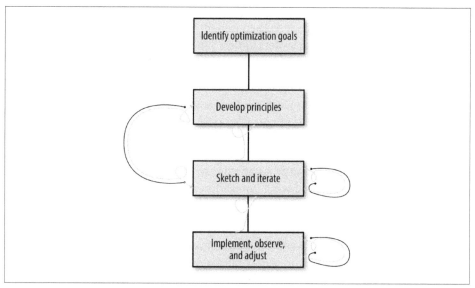

Figure 3-2. Microservice system design process

Set Optimization Goals

The behavior of your microservice system is "correct" when it helps you achieve your goals. There isn't a set of optimization goals that perfectly apply to all organizations, so one of your first tasks will be to identify the goals that make sense for your particular situation. The choice you make here is important—every decision in the design process after this is a trade-off made in favor of the optimization goal.

Note that optimization doesn't mean that other system qualities are undesirable. In fact, it is extremely likely that you will initially list many desirable outcomes for the system you create. But as you go through the system design process you will find that it is difficult to pull your system into many directions at the same time. A smaller set of optimization goals is easier to design for. A single optimization goal (like the

Vision Zero goal of zero traffic-related fatalities) provides the most clarity and has a higher likelihood of succeeding.

For example, a financial information system might be optimized for reliability and security above all other factors. That doesn't mean that changeability, usability, and other system qualities are unimportant—it simply means that the designers will always make decisions that favor security and reliability above all other things.

In Chapter 4 we will identify the goals that we have most commonly seen among companies that have embraced the microservices way and the principles that help support them.

 It is possible that you may need to change your optimization goals at some point in the lifetime of your application. That is OK; it just means that you need to follow the design process and implement small changes to guide your system toward the new goal. If the goal change is quite different from your original design goal this may take some time. If the optimization goal is radically different from your original goal, you may even create a new system design entirely.

Development Principles

Underpinning a system optimization goal is a set of principles. Principles outline the general policies, constraints, and ideals that should be applied universally to the actors within the system to guide decision-making and behavior. The best designed principles are simply stated, easy to understand, and have a profound impact on the system they act upon.

In Chapter 4 we will look at some of the principles that Netflix employs toward its optimization goals.

Sketch the System Design

If you find yourself building the application in a *greenfield* environment with no existing organization or solution architecture in place, it is important that you establish a good starting point for your system design. You won't be able to create the perfect system on your first try and you aren't likely to have the time or information to do that anyway. Instead, a good approach is to sketch the important parts of your system design for the purposes of evaluation and iteration.

How you do this is entirely up to you. There is a wealth of modeling and communication tools available to conceptualize organizational and solution architectures; choose the ones that work well for you. But the value of this step in the design process is to serialize some of the abstract concepts from your head into a tangible form that can be evaluated. The goal of a sketching exercise is to continually improve the design until you are comfortable moving forward.

The goal is to sketch out the core parts of your system, including organizational structure (how big are the teams? what is the direction of authority? who is on the team?), the solution architecture (how are services organized? what infrastructure must be in place?), the service design (what outputs? how big?), and the processes and tools (how do services get deployed? what tools are necessary?). You should evaluate these decisions against the goals and principles you've outlined earlier. Will your system foster those goals? Do the principles make sense? Do the principles need to change? Does the system design need to change?

Sketching is powerful when the risk of starting over is small. Good sketches are easy to make and easy to destroy, so avoid modeling your system in a way that requires a heavy investment of time or effort. The more effort it takes to sketch your system the less likely you are to throw it away. At this early stage of system design, change should be cheap.

Most importantly, remember that the purpose of the iterative sketching stage is to participate in the *process* of designing. The goal is to form new ideas, consider the impact of proposed designs, and experiment in a safe way. The goal is not to create a set of beautiful design documents or prescriptive plans.

Implement, Observe, and Adjust

Bad designers make assumptions about how a system works, apply changes in the hope that it will produce desired behavior, and call it a day. Good designers make small system changes, assess the impact of those changes, and continually prod the system behavior toward a desired outcome. But a good design process is predicated on your ability to get feedback from the system you are designing. This is actually much more difficult than it sounds—the impact of a change to one small part of the system may result in a ripple of changes that impact other parts of your system with low visibility.

The perfect microservice system provides perfect information about all aspects of the system across all the domains of culture, organization, solution architecture, services, and process. Of course, this is unrealistic. It is more realistic to gain *essential* visibility into our system by identifying a few key measurements that give us the most valuable information about system behavior. In organizational design, this type of metric is known as a key performance indicator (KPI). The challenge for the microservice designer is to identify the right ones.

Gathering information about your system by identifying KPIs is useful, but being able to utilize those metrics to predict future behavior is incredibly valuable. One of the challenges that all system designers face is the uncertainty about the future. With perfect information about how our system might need to change we could build boundaries in exactly the right places and make perfect decisions about the size of our services and teams.

Without perfect information we are forced to make assumptions. Designers working on existing applications can observe the existing and past behavior of the system to identify patterns—components that change often, requirements that are always in flux, and services that can expect high usage. But designers who are working on new applications often have very little information to start with—the only way to identify the brittle points of the application is to ship the product and see what happens.

The risk of making poor decisions is that we steer the system in a direction that increases our "technical debt" (i.e., the future cost of addressing a technical deficiency). If we go too far along the wrong path we risk producing a system that becomes too expensive to change, so we give up.

The classic microservices example of this is the cautionary tale of the "monolith." A team creates an initial release of an application when the feature set is small and the componentry has low complexity. Over time, the feature set grows and the complexity of the deployed application grows, making change ever more difficult. At this point, the team agrees that the application needs to be redesigned and modularized to improve its changeability. But the redesign work is continually deferred because the cost of that work is too high and difficult to justify.

At the other end of the scale is a system that is so overdesigned and overengineered for future flexibility that it becomes impractical. An incredibly complex, adaptable system that is built for massive amounts of change that never seems to happen.

Rather than trying to predict the future, a good microservices designer examines the current state and makes small, measurable changes to the system. This is a bit like taking a wrong turn on a long road trip—if you don't know that you've made a mistake you might not find out you're going the wrong way until it is too late to turn back. But if you have a navigator with you, they may inform you right away and you can take corrective action.

When you are driving a car, taking a corrective action to steer your car back in the right direction is fairly straightforward, but what should a corrective action look like in a microservices system? A system that is designed with a high degree of visibility might give us a lot of information about what is happening, but if the cost of changing the system is too high we won't be able to make any course corrections. This problem of costly change presents itself when you need special permission, additional funds, more people, or more time to make the changes you want to the system.

So, in order to design a microservice system that is dynamic you'll need to identify the right KPIs, be able to interpret the data, and make small, cheap changes to the system that can guide you back on the right course. This is only possible if the right organization, culture, processes, and system architecture are in place to make it cheap and easy to do so.

The Microservices System Designer

Throughout this chapter we've referred to the work that the microservices system designer needs to undertake. But we haven't identified who this system designer is or where she might fit into your existing organization.

To be most effective, the microservices system designer should be able to enact change to a wide array of system concerns. We've already identified that organization, culture, processes, solution architecture, and services are significant concerns for the system designer. But the boundaries of this *system* haven't been properly identified.

You could decide that the system boundaries should mirror the boundaries of the company. This means that the changes you enact could have a broad-reaching impact. Alternatively, you could focus on a particular team or division within the company and build a system that aligns with the parent company's strategic goals. In fact, this type of nested set of systems is fairly common and we see it all around us in the physical world (e.g., consider the complex systems of the human brain, the human, and the human community).

Ultimately, the microservices system designer or software system designer is responsible for all the elements of the bounded system. The implication is that there is a world within the system and world outside of these borders. The system designer's task is to introduce small changes within the system in order to produce behavior that will align with the desired goal. Not very different than the traditional executive, manager, or CIO's mission.

But outside of these managerial positions there aren't many roles in the technology domain that allow for this systematic solution view. Instead, responsibilities are segregated among specialists who may not share the same objectives: The solution architect focuses on the coordination of services, the team manager focuses on the people, and the service developer focuses on the service design. We believe that someone or some team must be responsible for the holistic view of the entire system for a microservices system to succeed.

Summary

In this chapter we introduced the microservices system model and a generic design process for influencing the system. Throughout the rest of the book we will be diving into each of the model's domains in much greater detail. Remember that each of the decisions you make about organizational design, culture, solution architecture, process, and automation can result in unintended consequences to the system as a whole. Always maintain your holistic perspective and continue to observe and adjust as required.

CHAPTER 4

Establishing a Foundation

Now that we have a general model for establishing complex systems, we also need to come up with goals, principles, and guidelines for actually designing the system. A common challenge in creating a microservice architecture for your company is finding the right set of principles to govern the work. One easy answer is to just *copy* someone else's successful model—to adopt the same goals, principles, and implementation patterns they used. This can work if the company you decide to mimic has the same general goals as your company. But that is not often the case. Each company has a unique set of priorities, culture, and customer challenges and simply taking on a fully formed model from some other organization is not likely to get you where you need to go.

In this chapter, we'll review a capabilities model for microservices environments. We'll also introduce the platform that represents the tools and services you provide your developer and operations teams to allow them to meet their objectives. The quality and fit of these tools has an important impact on your teams' productivity. We will also review how company culture—including team size—can affect the resulting output of your teams.

Following that, we'll focus on teams themselves; their size, communication modes, and the level of freedom they have to innovate within their own scope of work. There is quite a bit of research that shows that varying the size of the team has a direct impact on the quality of the code that team produces. And establishing support for creative thinking is another common trait for many of the companies we talked to in preparation for this book.

By the time you complete this chapter, you should have a better understanding of the role goals and principles have in establishing a successful microservice environment and how you can use platforms and innovation culture to improve the general output or your teams.

Goals and Principles

Regardless of the software architecture style you employ, it is important to have some overall *goals* and *principles* to help inform your design choices and guide the implementation efforts. This is especially true in companies where a higher degree of autonomy is provided to developer teams. The more autonomy you allow, the more guidance and context you need to provide to those teams.

In this section, we'll take a look at some general goals for a microservice architecture and some example principles. Along the way we'll list our own suggested principles for you to consider.

Goals for the Microservices Way

It is a good idea to have a set of high-level goals to use as a guide when making decisions about *what* to do and *how* to go about doing it. We've already introduced our ultimate goal in building applications in the microservices way: *finding the right harmony of speed and safety at scale*. This overarching goal gives you a destination to aim for and given enough time, iterations, and persistence, will allow you to build a system that hits the right notes for your own organization.

There is of course a glaring problem with this strategy—it might take a very long time for you to find that perfect harmony of speed and safety at scale if you are starting from scratch. But thanks to the efforts of generations of technologists we have access to proven methods for boosting both speed and safety. So, you don't need to reinvent established software development practices. Instead, you can experiment with the parameters of those practices.

From our research, we've been able to distill four specific goals that lead to practices that aid both safety and speed of change. These goals aren't unique to microservice architecture, but they are useful in shaping your journey. Here are the four goals to consider:

1. Reduce Cost: Will this reduce overall cost of designing, implementing, and maintaining IT services?

2. Increase Release Speed: Will this increase the speed at which my team can get from idea to deployment of services?

3. Improve Resilience: Will this improve the resilience of our service network?

4. Enable Visibility: Does this help me better *see* what is going on in my service network?

Let's look at these in a bit more depth.

Reduce cost

The ability to reduce the cost of designing, implementing, and deploying services allows you more flexibility when deciding whether to create a service at all. For example, if the work of creating a new service component includes three months of design and review, six months of coding and testing, and two more weeks to get into production, that's a very high cost—one that you would likely think very carefully about before starting. However, if creating a new service component takes only a matter of a few weeks, you might be more likely to build the component and see if it can help solve an important problem. Reducing costs can increase your agility because it makes it more likely that you'll experiment with new ideas.

In the operations world, reducing costs was achieved by virtualizing hardware. By making the cost of a "server" almost trivial, it makes it more likely that you can spin up a bunch of servers in order to experiment with load testing, how a component will behave when interacting with others, and so on. For microservices, this means coming up with ways to reduce the cost of coding and connecting services together. Templated component stubs, standardized data-passing formats, and universal interfaces are all examples of reducing the costs of coding and connecting service components.

Increase release speed

Increasing the speed of the "from design to deploy" cycle is another common goal. A more useful way to view this goal is that you want to *shorten* the time between idea and deployment. Sometimes, you don't need to "go faster," you just need to take a shortcut. When you can get from idea to running example quickly, you have the chance to get feedback early, to learn from mistakes, and iterate on the design more often before a final production release. Like the goal of reducing costs, the ability to increase speed can also lower the risk for attempting new product ideas or even things as simple as new, more efficient data-handling routines.

One place where you can increase speed is in the deployment process. By automating important elements of the deployment cycle, you can speed up the whole process of getting services into production. Some of the companies we talked with for this book spend a great deal of time building a highly effective deployment pipeline for their organization. Many of them have such a well-designed deployment model that they release to production multiple times a day (sometimes over 100 times a day!). Automating release can go a long way toward increasing the speed of your microservice implementation.

Improve resilience

No matter the speed or cost of solutions, it is also important to build systems that can "stand up" to unexpected failures. In other words, systems that don't crash, even when errors occur. When you have an overall system approach (not just focused on a single component or solution) you can aim for creating resilient systems. This goal is often much more reasonable than trying to create a single component that is totally free of bugs or errors. In fact, creating a component that will have zero bugs is often impossible and sometimes simply not worth the time and money it takes to try.

One of the ways DevOps practices has focused on improving resilience is through the use of automated testing. By making testing part of the build process, the tests are constantly run against checked-in code, which increases the chances of finding errors in the code. This covers the code, but not the errors that could occur at runtime. There are companies that run what they call *end-to-end* tests before releasing to production but many companies rely on a practice that Jez Humble calls blue-green deployment (*http://api.co/20Qs8mO*). In this case, a new release is placed in production with a small subset of users and, if all goes well during a monitoring phase, more users are routed to the new release until the full userbase is on the new release. If any problems are encountered during this phased rollout, the users can all be returned to the previous release until problems are resolved and the process starts again.

Enable visibility

Another key goal should be to enable runtime visibility. In other words, improve the ability of stakeholders to see and understand what is going on in the system. There is a good set of tools for enabling visibility during the coding process. We often get reports on the coding backlog, how many builds were created, the number of bugs in the system versus bug completed, and so on. But we also need visibility into the runtime system.

The DevOps practices of logging and monitoring are great examples of this level of runtime visibility. Etsy's John Allspaw has said, "If it moves graph it. If it matters, alert on it" (*http://api.co/allspaw-mtbf*). Most effort to date has been to log and monitor operation-level metrics (memory, storage, throughput, etc.). However, there are some monitoring tools that can take action when things go badly (e.g., reroute traffic).

Trade-offs

Each of these are important goals and sometimes they are competing goals. There are trade-offs to consider. You might be able to reduce your overall costs, but it might adversely affect runtime resilience. Or, you might be able to speed up deployment but that might mean you lose track of what services are running in production and reduce visibility into the larger service network. In the end, you'll need to *balance* various goals and find the right mix for your organization.

Your organization may have some other high-level goals you want to consider and document. Whatever these turn out to be, one of the next things you need to do is convert those goals into a set of actionable principles.

Operating Principles

Along with a set of goals for a microservice approach, it is important to have a set of *principles*. Unlike goals, which are general, principles offer more concrete guidance on how to act in order to achieve those goals. Principles are not rules—they don't set out *required* elements. Instead, they offer examples on how to act in identifiable situations. Principles can also be used to inform best practices. Many of the organizations we looked at when doing research have their own set of principles within their company.

Netflix

One company that has been open about their own journey toward creating a successful microservice architecture is Netflix. In 2013, Adrian Cockcroft, Netflix's Cloud Architect, presented a day-long workshop on Netflix's cloud architecture and operating principles.[1] We'll highlight a few of them here.

> We've called out just a few of Netflix's principles here. You can learn more about these and other key elements of the Netflix operating model by checking out the slides (*http://api.co/netflix-slides*) and video (*http://api.co/1NZhGIs*) from Adrian Cockcroft's 2013 talk, "Cloud Native Architecture." From 2014 on, Adrian left Netflix and has continued presenting on microservices, DevOps, and related technology issues. You can find these presentations and videos in a different SlideShare account (*http://slideshare.net/adrian cockcroft*).

Antifragility
  Netflix works to strengthen their internal systems so that they can withstand unexpected problems. "The point of antifragility is that you always want a bit of stress in your system to make it stronger." There are several things Netflix does to promote this, including their "Simian Army" set of tools, which "enforce architectural principles, induce various kinds of failures, and test our ability to survive them" (*http://api.co/1NZi1uE*). Software has bugs, operators make mistakes, and hardware fails. By creating failures in production under controlled conditions, developers are incentivized to learn to build more robust systems. Error reporting and recovery systems are regularly tested, and real failures are handled with minimal drama and customer impact.

---

1 *http://slideshare.net/adrianco* has better links and a full annotated Netflix architecture workshop deck that should be the basis for these references.

Immutability

Cockcroft says the principle of immutability is used at Netflix to assert that auto-scaled groups of service instances are stateless and identical, which enables Netflix's system to "scale horizontally." The Chaos Monkey, a member of the Simian Army, removes instances regularly to enforce the immutable stateless service principle. Another related technique is the use of "Red/Black pushes" (*http://api.co/1XJrY19*). Although each released component is immutable, a new version of the service is introduced alongside the old version, on new instances, then traffic is redirected from old to new. After waiting to be sure all is well, the old instances are terminated.

Separation of Concerns

The Netflix microservice architecture arises because of separation of concerns (SoC) in the engineering team organization. Each team owns a group of services. They own building, operating, and evolving those services, and present a stable agreed interface and service level agreement to the consumers of those services. Invoking Conway's law, an organization structured with independent self-contained cells of engineers will naturally build what is now called a microservice architecture.

So these are the three key principles: antifragility, immutability, and separation of concerns. Some of these same ideas were expressed in slightly different terms in 1978 by Douglas McIlroy when describing the Unix operating system.

Unix

A succinct set of software architecture principles appears in the foreword for the 1978 edition of Bell Labs' "UNIX Timesharing System" documentation (*http://api.co/25u0Rdd*). The four points (listed next) were offered as a set of "maxims that have gained currency among the builders and users of the Unix system."

Here is the list Douglas McIrloy and his colleagues called out:

1. Make each program do one thing well. To do a new job, build afresh rather than complicate old programs by adding new features.

2. Expect the output of every program to become the input to another, as yet unknown, program. Don't clutter output with extraneous information. Avoid stringently columnar or binary input formats. Don't insist on interactive input.

3. Design and build software, even operating systems, to be tried early, ideally within weeks. Don't hesitate to throw away the clumsy parts and rebuild them.

4. Use tools in preference to unskilled help to lighten a programming task, even if you have to detour to build the tools and expect to throw some of them out after you've finished using them.

One of the interesting things about these four principles is that they offer general guidance on how to *think* about writing software. Phrases like "do one thing well" and "build software ... to be tried early" can lead developers to adopt what is known in the Unix world as "The Rule of Parsimony" when writing code ("only write a big program when nothing else will do"). This along with other Unix rules provides developers with a set of guidelines for which programming languages or libraries to use. These principles are also meant to shape developers' thinking.

Suggested principles

Having a set of principles to guide software developers and architects makes a lot of sense. As we learned from the story at the top of this chapter, the jaggedness principle applies here as well. There is no one set of principles that matches every company. Each organization needs to create a set that works for *their company*.

With this in mind, we offer a set of eight principles that reflects aspects of the other examples we've looked at so far. You can use these as starter material in putting together your own unique set for your company, or tune these until they fit.

Do one thing well
> Many microservice implementations adopt the essential message—"do one thing well," which leads to the challenge of deciding what constitutes "one thing" in your implementation. For some, "one thing" is managing user accounts. For others, "one thing" is finding a single user record. We'll get a chance to talk about *how* they decide where these types of boundaries are drawn for your organization in Chapter 5.

Build afresh
> The second part of McIlroy's first principle ("build afresh") is also important. Part of the Unix philosophy is to create a collection of powerful tools that are predictable and consistent over a long period of time. It is worth considering this as an additional principle when implementing microservices. It may be better to build a *new* microservice component rather than attempt to take an existing component already in production and *change* it to do additional work. This also maps to Netflix's immutability principle.

Expect output to become input
> Another important principle for Unix developers is the notion that one program's output is another program's input. For Unix systems, this leads to reliance on text strings as the primary data-passing medium. On the Web, the data-passing medium is the media type (HTML, HAL, Siren, Collection+JSON, etc.). In some cases, you can even use HTTP's content-negotiation feature to allow API providers and consumers to decide for themselves *at runtime* which format will be used to pass data.

Don't insist on interactive input

In the Unix world, there is a desire to create scripts that tie a number of command-line tools together to create a "solution." This means humans don't need to be engaged every step of the way—the scripts handle both the input and the output on their own. Reducing the need for human interaction increases the likelihood that the component can be used in unexpected ways.

Human interaction isn't something that microservice components need to deal with at runtime. But when we expand our scope of focus to the microservice system, it's easy to find countless human interactions that could benefit from this principle. Reducing the dependency on human interaction in the software development process can go a long way toward increasing the speed at which change occurs.

Try early

Adopting the point of view that your microservice components should be "tried early" fits well with the notion of continuous delivery and the desire to have *speed* as a goal for your implementations. Another advantage of this "try early" principle is you will learn your mistakes early. It turns out "try early" is also a way to encourage teams to get in the habit of releasing early and often. The earlier you release (even when that release is to a test environment), the earlier you get feedback and the quicker you can improve.

Don't hesitate to throw it away

This is a difficult one for some developers. Being willing to throw something away can be hard when you've spent a great deal of time and effort building a component. However, when you adopt the "try early" principle, throwing away the early attempts is easier.

It is also important to consider this "throw it away" principle for components that have been running in production for a long time. Over time, components that did an important job may no longer be needed. You may have applied the "build afresh" principle and replaced this component with one that does the job better. It may be the case that the "one thing" that component does is simply no longer needed. The important thing is to be willing to throw away a component when it no longer serves its intended purpose.

Toolmaking

The "use tools" principle covers the notion that, when working to build a solution, you sometimes need to build the "right tool" for the job. One of the important elements in the developmental history of humans was the ability to create tools. These tools were created in order to reach a goal. In other words, tools are a *means*, not an end. This is also an important principle for microservice architecture.

While doing research for this book, we found several examples of companies that created their own developer and deployment tool chains in order to improve their overall developer experience. Sometimes these tools are built from existing open source software projects. Sometimes the tools are, themselves, passed into open source so that *others* can use them and contribute to improving and maintaining them. The important element here is to recognize that, in some cases, you may need to divert from building your *solution* and spend some time building tools to help you build that solution.

Platforms

Along with a set of general goals and concrete principles, you'll need tangible tools to make them real—a platform with which to make your microservice environment a reality. From a microservice architecture perspective, good platforms increase the harmonic balance between speed and safety of change at scale. We typically think about speed and safety as opposing properties that require a trade-off to be made but the right tooling and automation give you an opportunity to cheat the trade-off.

For example, the principle of immutability primarily improves the safety of changes that are made to the system. There is also an inherent release cost for immutability as each deployable unit needs its own associated release mechanisms, infrastructure, and management. On its own, the added cost can reduce the speed at which changes can be made. However, the introduction of containerization tools like Docker make independent deployability easy and greatly reduce the associated costs. When immutability is combined with containerization, both speed and safety of changes are optimized, which may explain the rapid adoption of Docker in large organizations.

With a platform we pass from the conceptual world to the actual world. The good news is that there are many examples of companies establishing—and even sharing—their microservice platforms. The challenge is that it seems every company is doing this their own way, which presents some choices to anyone who wants to build their own microservice environment. Do you just select one of the existing OSS platforms? Do you try to purchase one? Build one from scratch?

It would be a mistake to just select one of the popular company's platforms and adopt it without careful consideration. Does this company provide the same types of services that mine does? Does this company optimize for the same things that mine will? Do we have similar staffing and training environments? Are our target customers similar (priorities, skills, desired outcomes, etc.)?

Instead of focusing on a single existing company's platform, we'll look at a general model for microservice platforms. One of the ones we like was described by Adrian Cockcroft in 2014 (*http://api.co/cockroft-dockercon*). He outlined a set of capabilities that he said all microservice implementations need to deal with, which he called "microservice concerns." We will divide them into two groups: shared capabilities and local capabilities.

Shared Capabilities

It's common in large enterprises to create a shared set of services for everyone to use. These are typically centered around the common infrastructure for the organization. For example, anything that deals with hardware (actual or virtual) falls into this category. Common database technologies (MySQL, Cassandra, etc.) and other software-implemented infrastructure is another example of shared services.

Shared capabilities are platform services that all teams use. These are standardized things like container technology, policy enforcement, service orchestration/interop, and data storage services. Even in large organizations it makes sense to narrow the choices for these elements in order to limit complexity and gain cost efficiencies. Essentially, these are all services that are provided to every team in the organization.

 It is important to note that shared services does not mean shared instance or shared data. Just because all the teams use a single type of data storage technology (e.g., Datomic, Mongo, Cassandra, and MySQL) does not mean they all use the same running instance of the data storage and all read and write from the same tables.

While shared capabilities offer potential cost savings they are ultimately rooted in the microservices goal of change safety. Organizations that highly value safety of changes are more likely to deploy centralized shared capabilities that can offer consistent, predictable results. On the other hand, organizations that desire speed at all costs are likely to avoid shared components as much as possible as it has the potential to inhibit the speed at which decentralized change can be introduced. In these speed-centric companies, capability reuse is less important than speed of delivery. As with all things in the microservices way you will need to experiment with different forms of shared capabilities to see what works best for your unique context.

The following is a quick rundown of what shared services platforms usually provide:

Hardware services

All organizations deal with the work of deploying OS- and protocol-level software infrastructure. In some companies there is a team of people who are charged with accepting shipments of hardware (e.g., 1-U servers), populating those machines with a baseline OS and common software for monitoring, health checks, etc., and then placing that completed unit into a rack in the "server room" ready for use by application teams.

Another approach is to virtualize the OS and baseline software package as a virtual machine (VM). VMs like Amazon's EC2 and VMWare's hypervisors are examples of this technology. VMs make it possible to automate most of the work of populating a "new machine" and placing it into production.

A more recent trend is the use of *containers* to solve this problem. Docker is the most popular player in this field. We'll talk more about Docker in Chapter 6. But there are others. CoreOS Rocket is one. By the time you read this there may be many more container products in the space.

Code management, testing, and deployment

Once you have running servers as targets, you can deploy application code to them. That's where code management (e.g., source control and review), testing, and (eventually) deployment come in. There are quite a few options for all these services and some of them are tied to the developer environment, especially testing.

Most microservice shops go to considerable lengths to automate this part of the process. For example, the Amazon platform offers automation of testing and deployment that starts as soon a developer checks in her code. Since the process of automation can be involved and posting to production can be risky, it is a good idea to treat this as a shared service that all teams learn to use.

Data stores

There are many data storage platforms available today, from classic SQL-based systems to JSON document stores on through graph-style databases such as Riak and Neo4J. It is usually not effective for large organizations to support all possible storage technologies. Even today, some organizations struggle with providing proper support for the many storage implementations they have onsite. It makes sense for your organization to focus on a select few storage platforms and make those available to all your developer teams.

Service orchestration

The technology behind service orchestration or service interoperability is another one that is commonly shared across all teams. There is a wide range of options here. Many of the flagship microservice companies (e.g., Netflix and Amazon) wrote their own orchestration platforms. We'll cover more on this in Chapter 5.

Security and identity

Platform-level security is another shared service. This often happens at the perimeter via gateways and proxies. Again, some companies have written their own frameworks for this; Netflix's Security Monkey (*http://api.co/security-monkey*) is an example. There are also a number of security products available. Shared identity services are sometimes actually external to the company. We'll talk more about this in Chapter 6.

Architectural policy

Finally, along with shared security, sometimes additional policy services are shared. These are services that are used to enforce company-specific patterns or models—often at runtime through a kind of inspection or even invasive testing. One example of policy enforcement at runtime is Netflix's "Simian Army"—a set of services designed to purposely cause problems on the network (simulate missing packets, unresponsive services, and so on) to test the resiliency of the system.

Another kind of policy tooling is one that standardizes the way outages or other mishaps are handled *after the fact*. These kinds of after-action reviews are sometimes called postmortems. For example, Etsy created (and open sourced) a tool for standardizing postmortems called Morgue (*https://github.com/etsy/morgue*). Whether in the form of runtime monitors or postmortem analysis, policy services ensure that varying teams adhere to the same guidance on how to handle both resiliency and security in their implementations.

Local Capabilities

Local capabilities are the ones that are selected and maintained at the team or group level. One of the primary goals of the local capabilities set is to help teams become more self-sufficient. This allows them to work at their own pace and reduces the number of blocking factors a team will encounter while they work to accomplish their goals. Also, it is common to allow teams to make their own determination on which developer tools, frameworks, support libraries, config utilities, etc., are best for their assigned job. Sometimes these tools are selected from a curated set of "approved" products. Sometimes these tools are created in-house (even by the same team). Often they are open source, community projects.

Finally, it is important that the team making the decision is also the one taking responsibility for the results. Amazon's Werner Vogels' describes it this way:

> You build it, you run it.
>
> —Werner Vogels, Amazon CTO

In small organizations, it is likely that the local capability elements will be the same for the entire company (e.g., the small startup is just a single team anyway). However, as the company grows, acquires new products, and expands into new technology and market spaces, forcing everyone to continue to use the same developer tools, routing implementations, etc., does not scale well. At that point, it makes sense to allow product groups to start making those decisions for themselves.

Most local capabilities services are ones that access and/or manipulate the shared service. For example, Netflix created a tool to make it easy for teams to spin up Amazon machine images (or AMIs) called Aminator (*http://api.co/ami-aminator*), and another tool to make deploying code to those cloud images (called Asgard (*http://api.co/1Ue6Kmw*)). Both of these tools make dealing with AMIs and deployments a "self-service" experience. Dev teams don't need to rely on someone else to spin up machines or install software on them—the team does that themselves.

Here's a rundown of the common local capabilities for microservice environments:

General tooling
A key local capability is the power to automate the process of rolling out, monitoring, and managing VMs and deployment packages. Netflix created Asgard and Aminator for this. A popular open source tool for this is Jenkins (*https://jenkins-ci.org/*).

Runtime configuration
A pattern found in many organizations using microservices is the ability roll out new features in a series of controlled stages. This allows teams to assess a new release's impact on the rest of the system (are we running slower?, is there an unexpected bug in the release?, etc.). Twitter's Decider configuration tool is used by a number of companies for this including Pinterest, Gilt, and Twitter. This tool lets teams use configuration files to route traffic from the "current" set of services to the "newly deployed" set of services in a controlled way. In 2014, Twitter's Raffi Kirkorian explained Decider and other infrastructure topics in an InfoQ interview (*http://www.infoq.com/articles/twitter-infrastructure*). Facebook created their own tool called Gatekeeper (*http://api.co/1PcBdWf*) that does the same thing. Again, placing this power in the hands of the team that wrote and released the code is an important local capability.

Service discovery
There are a handful of popular service discovery tools including Apache Zookeeper (*https://zookeeper.apache.org/*), CoreOS' etcd (*https://coreos.com/etcd/*), and HashiCorp's Consul (*https://www.consul.io/*). We'll cover the role of discovery tools in Chapter 6. These tools make it possible to build and release services that, upon install, register themselves with a central source, and then allow other services to "discover" the exact address/location of each other at runtime. This ability to abstract the exact location of services allows various teams to make changes to the location of their own service deployments without fear of breaking some other team's existing running code.

Request routing
Once you have machines and deployments up and running and discovering services, the actual process of handling requests begins. All systems use some kind of request-routing technology to convert external calls (usually over HTTP, Web-

Sockets, etc.) into internal code execution (e.g., a function somewhere in the codebase). The simplest form of request routing is just exposing HTTP endpoints from a web server like Apache, Microsoft IIS, NodeJS, and others. However, as service requests scale up, it is common to "front" the web servers with specialized routing proxies or gateways. Netflix created Zuul (*http://api.co/27ZatPd*) to handle their routing. There are popular open source services like Netty (*http://netty.io/*) (created by JBoss) and Twitter's Finagle (*https://twitter.github.io/finagle/*). We'll talk more about gateways in Chapter 6.

System observability

A big challenge in rapidly changing, distributed environments is getting a view of the running instances—seeing their failure/success rates, spotting bottlenecks in the system, etc. There are quite a few tools for this. Twitter created (and open sourced) Zipkin (*http://twitter.github.io/zipkin/*) for this task, and there are other similar frameworks that provide visibility into the state of the running system.

There is another class of observability tooling—those that do more than *report* on system state. These tools actually take action when things seem to be going badly by rerouting traffic, alerting key team members, etc. Netflix's Hystrix (*http://techblog.netflix.com/2012/11/hystrix.html*) is one of those tools. It implements a pattern known as the Circuit Breaker (*http://martinfowler.com/bliki/CircuitBreaker.html*) to improve the resiliency of running systems.

Culture

Along with establishing goals and principles and arming your organization with the right tools for managing platform, code, and runtime environments, there is another critical foundation element to consider—your company culture. Culture is important because it not only sets the tone for the way people behave inside an organization, but it also affects the output of the group. The code your team produces is the *result* of the culture.

But what *is* culture? Quite a bit has been written about culture in general—from many perspectives including anthropological as well as organizational. We'll focus on the organizational point of view here. In her 1983 paper, "Concepts of Culture and Organizational Analysis" (*http://api.co/smircich*), Linda Smircich describes culture as "shared key values and beliefs" that convey a sense of identity, generate commitment to something larger than the self, and enhances social stability.Damon Edwards of DTO Solutions and one of the organizers of the DevOpsDays series of events defines culture as "why we do it the way we do it" (*http://api.co/1qXA89l*).

So, how does culture affect team output? And, if it does, what kinds of team culture improve team performance and work quality? We'll look at three aspects of culture that you should consider as a foundation for your microservice efforts:

Communication
> Research shows that the way your teams communicate (both to each other and to other teams) has a direct measurable effect on the quality of your software.

Team alignment
> The size of your teams also has an effect on output. More people on the team means essentially more overhead.

Fostering innovation
> Innovation can be disruptive to an organization but it is essential to growth and long-term success.

Focus on Communication

One of the best-known papers on how culture affects team output is Mel Conway's 1968 article in *Datamation* magazine (*http://www.melconway.com/Home/Commit tees_Paper.html*), "How Do Committees Invent?" The line most often quoted from this short and very readable paper is:

> Organizations which design systems … are constrained to produce designs that are copies of the communication structures of these organizations.
>
> —Mel Conway, author of "How Do Committees Invent?"

Put simply, *communication dictates output.*

This quote was identified in 1975 by Fred Brooks as "Conway's law" and it provides some important insights on the importance of organizational structure affecting the quality of the final product of the company. Conway's paper identifies a number of reasons for this assertion as well as directives on how to leverage this understanding to improve the group's output. A 2009 study for Microsoft Research (*http://dl.acm.org/citation.cfm?id=1368160*) showed that "organizational metrics are significantly better predictors of error-proneness" in code than other more typical measures including code complexity and dependencies.

Another key point in Conway's article is that "the very act of organizing a team means certain design decisions have already been made." The process of deciding things like the size, membership, even the physical location of teams is going to affect the team choices and, ultimately, the team output. This gives a hint to the notion of applying Conway's law when setting up your team structure for a software project (sometimes referred to as a "reverse Conway"). By considering the communication needs and coordination requirements for a software project, you can set up your teams to make things easier, faster, and to improve overall communication.

Aligning Your Teams

Team alignment is important—it affects the quality of code. What can we do to take advantage of this information? Using the information from the start of this chapter, what "tunable" elements can we use to improve the alignment of our team structures to meet our goals for increasing speed, resilience, and visibility for our microservice efforts?

In his 1998 paper, "The Social Brain" (*http://api.co/social-brain*), British anthropologist Robin Dunbar found that social group sizes fall into predictable ranges. "[T]he various human groups that can be identified in any society seem to cluster rather tightly around a series of values (5, 12, 35, 150, 500, and 2,000)." These groups each operate differently. The first (5) relies very much on a high-trust, low-conversation mode: they seem to understand each other without lots of discussion. Dunbar found that, as groups get larger, more time is spent on maintaining group cohesion. In his book *Grooming, Gossip and the Evolution of Language* (*http://api.co/dunbar-evolution*), Dunbar suggests that in large primate groups up to 40% of time is spent in grooming just to maintain group stability. He points out that this grooming behavior in primates is replaced by gossip and other trivial conversations in humans.

Dunbar's "grooming" in primates is analogous to meetings, emails, and other forms of communication in organizations that are often seen as time wasters. The possibility of increasing the number of internal meetings with large groups at Amazon in the early days of their AWS services implementation prompted Jeff Bezos to quip:

> No, communication is terrible!
>
> —Jeff Bezos, Amazon founder and CEO

This led to Bezos' now famous "two-pizza team" rule. Any team that cannot be fed by two pizzas is a team that is too big.

Fred Brooks' 1975 book *The Mythical Man Month* contains the classic observation that "adding [more people] to a late software project makes it later." This maxim speaks directly to the notion that adding people increases communication overhead, similar to the findings of Dunbar.

As the size of the group grows, the number of unique communication channels grows in a nonlinear way. This instance of *combinatorial explosion* is a common problem and needs to be kept in mind as you design your teams.

When we talk to companies working in the microservices way, they commonly cite team sizes that match closely to Dunbar's first two groups (5 and 12). We refer to these as Dunbar levels 1 and 2, respectively. For example, Spotify, the Swedish music streaming company, relies on a team size of around seven (what they call a [squad (*http://api.co/1TSPVld*)). They also rely on an aggregate of several teams that they call a tribe and reference Dunbar's work directly when describing how they came to this arrangement.

There are a number of other factors in establishing your teams including responsibilities, deliverables, and skillsets that need to be present within a team. We'll cover details on how to go about selecting and tuning these elements later in the book.

Fostering Innovation

A third important element in managing company culture is fostering innovation within your organization. Many companies say they want to make innovative thinking common within the organization. And the ability to take advantage of creative and innovative ideas is sometimes cited as a reason to adopt a microservice approach to developing software. So it makes sense to spend a bit of time exploring what innovation looks like and how it can affect your organization.

A simple definition of *innovate* from Merriam-Webster's dictionary is "to do something in a new way; to have new ideas about how something can be done." It's worth noting that *being innovative* is most often focused on changing something that is already established. This is different than *creating* something new. Innovation is usually thought of as an opportunity to improve what a team or company already has or is currently doing.

A common challenge is that the innovation process can be very disruptive to an organization. Sometimes "changing the way we do things" can be seen as a needless or even threatening exercise—especially if the change will disrupt some part of the organization (e.g., result in eliminating tasks, reducing workload, or even replacing whole teams). For this reason, the act of innovating can be difficult. Another problem with innovation is that the actual *process* often looks chaotic from the outside. Innovating can mean coming up with ideas that might not work, that take time to get operating properly, or even start out as more costly and time consuming than the current practice. Yet, many organizations really *want* to encourage innovative work within their teams.

Companies we talked to enable innovation by adopting a few key principles. First, they provide a level of autonomy to their teams. They allow teams to determine the best way to handle details *within* the team. Netflix calls this the principle of "context, not control." Team leaders are taught to provide context for the team's work and guidance on meeting goals, but to *not* control what the team does. Netflix's Steve Urban explains it like this (*http://api.co/27ZaylY*):

> I have neither the place, the time, nor the desire, to micromanage or make technical decisions for [my team].
>
> —Steve Urban, Netflix engineer

Second, companies that foster innovation build in a tolerance for some level of chaos. They operate with the understanding that it's OK if some things look a bit disorganized or messy. Of course, there are limits to this. *Harvard Business Review*'s "Managing Innovation: Controlled Chaos" (*http://api.co/1Z8BcCR*) points out that "Effective managers of innovation … administer primarily by setting goals, selecting key people, and establishing a few critical limits and decision points for intervention." Fostering innvotation means setting boundaries that prevent teams from taking actions that threaten the health and welfare of the company and allowing teams to act on their own within these safe boundaries.

Managing communication channels, aligning teams, and establishing a safe place to innovate are all essential to enabling a successful culture that can take advantage of a microservice-style approach to designing, implementing, and maintaining software.

Summary

In this chapter we've reviewed the common set of platform capabilities called Cockcroft's "microservices concerns" and cited examples of how a number of organizations provide these platform capabilities to their teams. We also focused on the teams themselves. The way your teams communicate, their size, and the level of innovation you support within those teams have a significant effect on the quality of their output.

So, with these ideals in mind, what does it take to actually *implement* microservice solutions? In the next two chapters we'll show you working examples of the platform capabilities we discussed here as well as offer guidance on component design and implementation that follows the recommended principles from this chapter.

PART III

Microservices in Practice

The Microservices Way at Hootsuite

Vancouver-based Hootsuite is a pioneer in social media for business. The company was formed by members of Invoke Media who built a platform to manage their own social network interactions and then realized that other companies had the same need. As the company grew, so did their monolithic, PHP-based platform. In order to meet the demands of their market through a 100+ team of developers, they are evolving their application to a collection of product-oriented microservices (*http://api.co/ 1U7Z5Xa*).

Hootsuite took a design-based approach to their microservice migration from the outset. They recognized that defining the right logic boundaries can be a harder problem than introducing new technology. They use what they call "distributed domain-driven design" as a means of breaking services out of their monolith. API definitions and associated contracts provide a means of describing service scope and function, and API consumers are involved in the creation of both. The Hootsuite team found that API design guidelines helped to create a common language for this process. Over time, Hootsuite has classified their microservices into three categories: data services that encapsulate key business entities and ensure scalability, functional services that combine data services with business logic to execute core business logic, and facade services that decouple consumer contracts from core functional logic. Hootsuite's design approach continues to evolve as their microservice implementation matures.

Hootsuite's organization includes product-aligned teams made up of five to seven people. They also have a cross-functional platform team that is responsible for frameworks and tooling, and has visibility across the organization. To address common interest areas like APIs and JavaScript, they have a collection of "guilds" that anyone can join. In the spirit of empowerment and delivery speed, Hootsuite does not have any governance checkpoints that intrude on a team's development process. Instead, they have a set of community-defined principles and tools that guide microservice development. Recently, they formed a technology architecture group made up of senior technical leaders to address technological issues that have a broad effect on the organization, but this group was formed organically—not as the result of an executive edict. Beier Cai, Director of Software Development, likens Hootsuite's governance approach to "eventual consistency." This empowered, iterative style is a match for the microservices way.

Fittingly given the company's origin, Hootsuite has created a goal-oriented toolset for microservices. To address deployment, they use Docker and Mesos. For service discovery, they use Consul and NGINX. These four open source components are used together in a solution called "Skyline" that enables secure, dynamic, performant routing in their growing fabric of microservices. They have also found Scala, Akka, and the Play framework useful in building their individual services, and leverage both HTTP and Kafka for interservice communication. The tooling extends to the design process as well. To make sure developers know what services and components are available for use in service development, the Hootsuite team created a tool to dynamically generate system visualizations that link to code repositories and operational documentation. As needs arise, more tools are discovered or created.

Hootsuite's evolution to a microservice architecture continues. They have over a dozen microservices in production with many more on the way. As a result of embracing an approach to microservices adoption that cuts across their architecture, organization, culture, processes, and tools, they have been able to improve their delivery speed, flexibility, autonomy, and developer morale.

CHAPTER 5

Service Design

As discussed in Chapter 3, one of the key elements—the one most everyone thinks of when we talk about microservice architecture—is the design of the actual microservice components themselves. It is these autonomous services that make up the fabric of our microservice system and do the actual work of implementing your solution strategy. Implementing systems that contain a large number of small service components is a challenge so we'll devote an entire chapter to a set of tools and processes that can help you and your team take on the task.

In our experience working with various organizations and interviewing others, some of the more challenging questions that teams adopting microservice architecture face are how to properly size microservices ("how micro is *micro*?") and how to properly deal with data persistence in order to avoid sharing of data across services. These two concerns are actually closely related. A mistake in optimal sizing often begets the extraneous data-sharing problem, but the latter is especially problematic, operationally, since it can create tight cross-service coupling and impede independent deployability, a core value of the architectural style. Other topics that come up frequently when we talk with people who are designing and implementing microservices are things like support for asynchronous messaging, transaction modeling, and dealing with dependencies in a microservice environment. Getting a handle on these elements will help you curb the amount of additional (nonessential) complexity that creeps into your overall system. And doing that can help you in your constant struggle to balance the two key factors in any IT system: speed and safety.

In this chapter, we will cover microservice boundaries, looking at just how "micro" a service should be and why. We will explore microservice interfaces (APIs), discussing the importance of evolvable, message-oriented APIs for microservices and how they can reduce intercomponent coupling. We will investigate effective data storage approaches for microservices, exploring the power of shifting from data-centric and state-capturing models toward capability-driven and event-sourcing-oriented ones. We'll also show how the command query responsibility segregation (CQRS) pattern can improve the granularity of data services, while maintaining sufficient speed and safety.

This chapter will also cover key topics such as supporting transactions across microservice boundaries, asynchronous messaging, and dealing with dependencies with eyes on the prize of independent deployability.

By the time we get through this material you should have a good understanding of the challenges as well as the available patterns and practices you can use when it comes to designing and building microservice components.

Let's get started with the big one: "What is the optimal size of a microservice?"

Microservice Boundaries

So just how micro should a microservice be?

In reality, there is no simple answer for this question. The things that first come to mind, such as lines of code in a microservice or the size of a team working on one are compelling, since they offer the chance to focus on a *quantifiable* value (e.g., "The answer is 42!").[1] However, the problem with these measures is that they ignore the business context of what we are implementing. They don't address the organizational context of who is implementing the service and, more importantly, how the service is being used within your system.

Instead of trying to find some quantity to measure, we find most companies focus on a *quality* of each microservice—the use case or context in which the component will be used. Many microservice adopters have turned to Eric Evans' "domain-driven design" (DDD) approach for a well-established set of processes and practices that facilitate effective, business-context–friendly modularization of large complex systems.

Microservice Boundaries and Domain-Driven Design

Essentially, what we see people doing when they introduce the microservices way into their companies is that they begin to decompose existing components into smaller parts in order to increase their ability to improve the quality of the service faster without sacrificing reliability.

There are many ways to decompose a large system into smaller subsystems. In one case we may be tempted to decompose a system based on implementation technology.

---

[1] *http://api.co/1WtSZGE*

For instance, we can say that all computationally heavy services need to be written in C or Rust or Go (choose your own poison) and therefore they are a separate subsystem, while I/O-heavy features could certainly benefit from the nonblocking I/O of a technology such as Node.js and therefore they are a subsystem of their own. Alternatively, we can divide a large system based on team geography: one subsystem may be written in the US, while others may be developed and maintained by software teams in Africa, Asia, Australia, Europe, or South America. Intuitively, giving a self-contained subsystem for development to a team that is located in one place is well-optimized. Another reason you may decide to divide a system based on geography is that specific legal, commercial, and cultural requirements of operating in a particular market may be better understood by a local team. Can a software development team from New York accurately capture all the necessary details of an accounting software that will be used in Cairo?

In his seminal book *Domain-Driven Design*, Eric Evans outlines a fresh approach to determining boundaries of subsystems in the context of a larger system. In the process, he offers a model-centric view of software system design. As we've pointed out in this book, models are a great way to view a system. They provide an abstract way to look at something—a way that highlights the things we are interested in. Models are a point of view.

It's Only a Model

To understand the DDD approach, it is important to remember that any software system is a model of a reality—it is not the reality itself. For instance, when we log in to online banking and are looking at our checking account, we are not looking at the actual checking account. We're just looking at a representation—a model—that gives us information about the checking account such as balance and past transactions. It's likely that the screen our bank teller sees when looking at our account has different information because it's another model of our account.

In his book, Evans notes that most large systems don't actually have a single model. The overall model of a large system is actually comprised of many smaller models that are intermingled with each other. These smaller models are organic representations of relevant business contexts—they make sense in their context and when used within the context they are intuitive for a person who is the subject matter expert of the context.

Bounded Context

In DDD, Evans points out that teams need to be very careful when combining contextual models to form a larger software system. He puts it this way:

> Multiple models are in play on any large project. Yet when code based on distinct models is combined, software becomes buggy, unreliable, and difficult to understand. Communication among team members becomes confused. It is often unclear in what context a model should not be applied.
>
> —Eric Evans, author of *Domain-Driven Design: Tackling Complexity in the Heart of Software*

It is worth noting that Evans' DDD was introduced more than a decade before the word "microservice" had come into vogue. Yet, the preceding quotation is an important observation about the nature of modeling—if you try to rely on a single model (e.g., a canonical model) things become difficult to understand. The microservices way attempts to break large components (models) into smaller ones in order to reduce the confusion and bring more clarity to each element of the system. As such, microservice architecture is an architectural style that is highly compatible with the DDD way of modeling. To aid in this process of creating smaller, more coherent components, Evans introduced the bounded contexts concept. Each component in the system lives within its own bounded context, which means the model for each component and these context models are only used within their bounded scope and are not shared across the bounded contexts.

It is generally acknowledged that properly identifying bounded contexts in a system, using DDD techniques, and breaking up a large system along the seams of those bounded contexts is an effective way of designing microservice boundaries. In his book *Building Microservices*, Sam Newman states:

> If our service boundaries align to the bounded contexts in our domain, and our microservices represent those bounded contexts, we are off to an excellent start in ensuring that our microservices are loosely coupled and strongly cohesive.

Newman makes an important point here: bounded contexts represent autonomous business domains (i.e., distinct business capabilities), and therefore are the appropriate starting point for identifying the dividing lines for microservices. If we use the DDD and bounded contexts approaches, the chances of two microservices needing to share a model and the corresponding data space, or ending up having tight coupling, are much lower. Avoiding data sharing improves our ability to treat each microservice as an independently deployable unit. And independent deployability is how we can increase our speed while still maintaining safety within the overall system.

Using DDD and bounded contexts is an excellent process for designing components. However, there is more to the story. We could actually use DDD and still end up creating fairly large components. But large is not what we're going for in a microservice architecture. Instead, we're aiming at small—micro, even. And that leads to an important aspect of designing microservice components—smaller is better.

Smaller Is Better

The notion of work-unit granularity is a crucial one in many contexts of modern software development. Whether defined explicitly or implicitly, we can clearly see the trend showing up in such foundational methodologies as Agile Development, Lean Startup, and Continuous Delivery (*http://api.co/deploy-line*), among others. These methodologies have revolutionized project management, product development, and DevOps, respectively.

It is interesting to note that each one of them has the principle of size reduction at its core: reducing the size or scope of the problem, reducing the time it takes to complete a task, reducing the time it takes to get feedback, and reducing the size of the deployment unit. These all fall into a notion we call "batch-size reduction."

For example, here's an excerpt from the Agile Manifesto (*http://www.agilemani festo.org/*):

> Deliver working software frequently, from a couple of weeks to a couple of months, with a preference to the shorter timescale.
>
> —The Agile Manifesto, Kent Beck et al.

Basically, moving to Agile from Waterfall can be viewed as a reduction of the "batch size" of a development cycle—if the cycle was taking many months in Waterfall, now we strive to complete a similar batch of tasks: define, architect, design, develop, and deploy, in much shorter cycles (weeks versus months). Granted, the Agile Manifesto lists other important principles as well, but they only reinforce and complement the core principle of "shorter cycles" (i.e., reduced batch size).

In the case of Lean Startup, Eric Ries directly points to the crucial importance of small batch size, right in the definition of the methodology:

> The Lean Startup takes its name from the lean manufacturing revolution that Taiichi Ohno and Shigeo Shingo are credited with developing at Toyota. Lean thinking is radically altering the way supply chains and production systems are run. Among its tenets are drawing on the knowledge and creativity of individual workers, the shrinking of batch sizes, just-in-time production and inventory control, and an acceleration of cycle times. It taught the world the difference between value-creating activities and waste and showed how to build quality into products from the inside out.
>
> —Eric Ries, author of *The Lean Startup*

Similarly, when discussing the principal benefits of Continuous Delivery (*http://martinfowler.com/bliki/ContinuousDelivery.html*), Martin Fowler is unambiguous about the role of small batch sizes, calling it the precondition for a core benefit of the methodology.

Once you adopt the notion of limited batch size from Agile, Lean, and Continuous Delivery at the code, project, and deployment level, it makes sense to think about applying it at the architecture level as well. And many of the companies we interviewed have done this. After all, architecture is the direct counterpart to the other three disciplines. So, in the simplest terms, this "limited batch size" is the "micro" in microservice.

 Just as in Agile, etc., there's no simple, universal measure for determining just "how small" a microservice should be (e.g., a quantity). What people tell us is that they use the word "small" as a quality like "reliable" and "coherent," etc.

Ubiquitous Language

Just by stating a simple preference of "smaller is better," we immediately run into a problem if bounded contexts are our only tool for sizing microservices, because bounded contexts cannot actually be arbitrarily small. Here's what one of the prominent authorities in the space of DDD, Vaughn Vernon, had to say about the optimal size of a bounded context:

> Bounded context should be as big as it needs to be in order to fully express its complete ubiquitous language.
>
> —Vaughn Vernon, author of *Implementing Domain–Driven Design*

In DDD, we need a shared understanding and way of expressing the domain specifics. This shared understanding should provide business and tech teams with a common language that they can use to collaborate on the definition and implementation of a model. Just as DDD tells us to use one model within a component (the bounded context), the language used within that bounded context should be coherent and pervasive—what we in DDD call ubiquitous language.

From a purely technical perspective, the smaller the microservice the easier it can be developed quicker (Agile), iterated on quicker (Lean), and deployed more frequently (Continuous Delivery). But on the modeling side, it is important to avoid creating services that are "too small." According to Vernon, we cannot arbitrarily reduce the size of a bounded context because its optimal size is determined by the business context (model). Our technical need for the size of a service can sometimes be different (smaller) from what DDD modeling can facilitate. This is probably why Sam Newman, very carefully, called bounded context analysis an "excellent start," but not the sole prescription for how to size microservices. And we completely agree. Bounded contexts are a great start, but we need more tools in our toolbelt if we are to size microservices efficiently. We will discuss some of those tools later in this chapter, in particular when we look into data storage for microservices.

API Design for Microservices

When considering microservice component boundaries, the source code itself is only part of our concern. Microservice components only become valuable when they can communicate with other components in the system. They each have an interface or API. Just as we need to achieve a high level of separation, independence, and modularity of our code we need to make sure that our APIs, the component interfaces, are also loosely coupled. Otherwise, we won't be able to deploy two microservices independently, which is one of our primary goals in order to balance speed and safety.

We see two practices in crafting APIs for microservices worth mentioning here:

- Message-oriented
- Hypermedia-driven

Messsage-Oriented

Just as we work to write component code that can be safely refactored over time, we need to apply the same efforts to the shared interfaces between components. The most effective way to do this is to adopt a message-oriented implementation for microservice APIs. The notion of messaging as a way to share information between components dates back to the initial ideas about how object-oriented programming would work. Alan Kay reminded everyone of the power of messages on an email list in 1998 (*http://api.co/kay-systems*):

> I'm sorry that I long ago coined the term "objects" for this topic because it gets many people to focus on the lesser idea. The big idea is "messaging."
>
> —Alan Kay

All of the companies we talked with about microservice component design mentioned the notion of messaging as a key design practice. For example, Netflix relies on message formats like Avro, Protobuf, and Thrift over TCP/IP for communicating internally (*http://api.co/1U7ZgBX*) and JSON over HTTP for communicating to external consumers (e.g., mobile phones, browsers, etc.). By adopting a message-oriented approach, developers can expose general entry points into a component (e.g., an IP address and port number) and receive task-specific messages at the same time. This allows for changes in message content as a way of refactoring components safely over time. The key lesson learned here is that for far too long, developers have viewed APIs and web services as tools to transmit serialized "objects" over the wire. However, a more efficient approach is to look at a complex system as a collection of services exchanging messages over a wire.

Hypermedia-Driven

Some companies we spoke to are taking the notion of message-oriented to the next level. They are relying on hypermedia-driven implementations. In these instances, the messages passed between components contain more than just data. The messages also contain descriptions of possible actions (e.g., links and forms). Now, not just the data is loosely coupled—so are the actions. For example, Amazon's API Gateway and App-Stream APIs both support responses in the Hypertext Application Language (HAL) format (*http://stateless.co/hal_specification.html*).

Hypermedia-style APIs (*http://api.co/1VqvjC2*) embrace evolvability and loose coupling as the core values of the design style. You may also know this style as APIs with Hypermedia As The Engine Of Application State (HATEOAS APIs). Regardless of the name used, if we are to design proper APIs in microservice architecture, it helps to get familiar with the hypermedia style.

Hypermedia style is essentially how HTML works for the browser. HTTP messages are sent to an IP address (your server or client location on the Internet) and a port number (usually "80" or "443"). The messages contain the data and actions encoded in HTML format. For example, a message that contains information on an outstanding shipment due to arrive at your office might look like this:

```html
<html>
  <head>
    <title>Shipment #123</title>
  </head>
  <body>
    <h1>Shipment #123</h1>
    <div id="data">
      <span>ID: 123</span><br />
      <span>Description: Widget Covers</span><br />
      <span>Quantity: 1 Gross</span><br />
      <span>Estimated Arrival: 2017-01-09</span><br />
    </div>
    <div id="actions">
      <a href="...">Refresh</a>
      <a href="...">Exit</a>
      <form method="get" action="...">
        <input name="id" value="" />
        <input type="submit" value="Search" />
      </form>
    </div>
  </html>
```

James Gregory of ThoughtWorks, a company experienced in helping customers adopt and implement microservice-style systems, puts it this way (*http://api.co/1NZkTIb*):

When we work on projects with more and more services involved the big revelation was the people who build HTTP and use Hypermedia know what they're talking about —and we should listen to them.

—James Gregory, Lead Consultant at ThoughtWorks

The hypermedia API style is as transformative to the API space as object-oriented design was for code design. A long time ago, we used to just write endless lines of code (maybe lightly organizing them in functions), but then object-oriented design came by with a revolutionary idea: "what if we grouped the state and the methods that operate on that state in an autonomous unit called *an object*, thus encapsulating data and behavior?" In essence, hypermedia style has very similar approach but for API design. This is an API style in which API messages contain both data and *controls* (e.g., metadata, links, forms), thus dynamically guiding API clients by responding with not just static data but also control metadata describing API affordances (i.e., "what can I do with this API?").

To learn more about hypermedia APIs and how to design them, check out the book *RESTful Web APIs* by Mike Amundsen, Leonard Richardson, and Sam Ruby. By the way, don't let the book title fool you—even though it says "RESTful," it is about hypermedia APIs and among other things explains why the book says REST while it talks about hypermedia APIs.

Exposing affordances makes sense for services that communicate over the Web. If we look at the Web as both the human-centric Web (websites consumed by humans) and machine Web (APIs), we can see stark differences in how far behind the machine Web is. When you load a web page on the human-centric Web, it doesn't just give you content (text, photos, videos, etc.)—most web pages also contain links to related content or search menus: something you can interact with. Basically, web pages tell you, in the response itself, what else you can do. Conventional web APIs don't do this. Most contemporary RESTful (CRUD) APIs respond with just data and then you have to go and read some documentation to find out what else can be done. Imagine if websites were like that: you would go to a specific URL, read content, then you'd have to look in some documentation (a book? a PDF?) to find other interesting URLs, many of which may be outdated, to navigate to the next thing. Most people would agree that it would be quite a ridiculous experience. The human Web wouldn't be very functional if the responses didn't contain behavioral affordances. But that's exactly the case for most modern RESTful APIs. And, as a matter of fact, the *data-only* approach is quite as brittle and dysfunctional for the machine Web as the picture we painted for the human-centric Web, except we have gotten used to the unfortunate state of affairs.

Hypermedia APIs are more like the human Web: evolvable, adaptable, versioning-free—when was the last time you cared about what "version" of a website you are looking at? As such, hypermedia-style APIs are less brittle, more discoverable, and fit right at home in a highly distributed, collaborative architectural style such as microservices.

Data and Microservices

As software engineers, we have been trained to think in terms of data, first and foremost. To give the simplest example, it has pretty much been ingrained in our "muscle memory," or whatever the mental equivalent of one is, to start system design by first designing the pertinent data models. When asked to build an application, the very first task most software engineers will complete is identifying entities and designing database tables for data storage. This is an efficient way of designing centralized systems and whole generations of programmers have been trained to think this way. But data-centric design is not a good way to implement distributed systems—especially systems that rely on independently deployable microservices. The biggest reason for this is the absence of strong, centralized, uniform control over the entire system in the case of distributed systems, which makes a formerly efficient process inefficient.

The first step in breaking the data-centric habit is to rethink our system designs. We need to stop designing systems as a collection of data services and instead use business capabilities as the design element, or as Sam Newman notes in his book:

> You should be thinking not in terms of data that is shared, but about the capabilities those contexts provide [...]. I have seen too often that thinking about data leads to anemic, CRUD-based (create, read, update, delete) services. So ask first "What does this context do?" and then "So what data does it need to do that?"
>
> —Sam Newman, author of *Building Microservices*

It turns out that capabilities-centric design is more suitable for microservices than a more traditional, data-centric design.

Shipping, Inc.

To demonstrate some of the practical aspects of microservice architecture, throughout Chapters 5 and 6 we will be using an imaginary startup. Let's assume that we are designing a microservice architecture for a fledgling shipment company, aptly named Shipping, Inc. As a parcel-delivery company, they need to accept packages, route them through various sorting warehouses (hops on the route), and eventually deliver to the destination. Because it is 2016 and the company is very tech-savvy, Shipping, Inc. is building native mobile applications for a variety of platforms to let customers track their packages all the way from pickup to final delivery. These mobile applications will get the data and functionality they need from a set of microservices.

Let's imagine that Shipping, Inc.'s accounting and sales subsystems (microservices) need access to daily currency exchange rates to perform their operations. A data-centric design would create a table or set of tables in a database that contain exchange rates. Then we would let various subsystems query our database to retrieve the data. This solution has significant issues—two microservices depend on the design of the shared table and data in it, leading to tight coupling and impeding independent deployability.

If instead, we had viewed "currency exchange rates" as a capability and had built an independent microservice (currency rates) serving the sales and accounting microservices, we would have had three independent services, all loosely coupled and independently deployable. Furthermore, since, by their nature, APIs in services hide implementation details, we can completely change the data persistence supporting the currency rates service (e.g., from MySQL to Cassandra, if scalability became an issue) without any of the service's consumers noticing the change or needing to adjust. Last but not least, since services (APIs) are able to put forward alternative interfaces to its various consumers, we can easily alter the interface that the currency rates microservice provides to the sales microservice, without affecting the accounting microservice, thus fulfilling the promise of independent evolution, a necessity for independent deployability. Mission accomplished!

Thinking in terms of capabilities rather than data is a very powerful technique for API design, in general. It usually results in a more use-case-oriented interface (instead of an SQL-like data-object interface). A capabilities-centric API design is usually a good approach, but in the case of microservices it is not just a smart design technique, it's a powerful way of avoiding tight coupling. We just saw evidence of this.

Much like bounded context analysis, capabilities-oriented design is a crucial technique but not sufficient to ensure independent deployability for all use cases. Not every example is as simple as our currency rates one. We cannot always encapsulate shared data inside a microservice and call it a day. For example, a common use case that cannot be solved with encapsulated capabilities is that of reporting. Any business application requires a certain level of reporting. And reporting often spans across multiple models, bounded contexts, and capabilities. Should reporting-oriented microservices be allowed to share tables with other microservices? The obvious answer is no, because that would immediately create severe tight coupling of services all around the system, and at the very least undermine (if not completely kill) independent deployability.

Let's see what techniques we can use to avoid data-sharing in complex use cases. The first one we will look at is *event sourcing*, a powerful data-modeling methodology that can help us avoid data-sharing in microservices, even in very complicated cases. The second, related methodology is CQRS—command query responsibility segregation.

Event Sourcing

We've mentioned that there are some deeply ingrained software engineering habits that greatly affect the way we typically approach systems engineering. One of the most widespread of those habits is structural data modeling. It has become very natural for us to describe models as collections of interacting logical entities and then to map those logical entities to physical tables where the data is stored. More recently, we have started using NoSQL and object stores that take us slightly away from the relational world, but in essence the approach is still the same: we design structural entities that model objects around us and then we "save" the object's state in a database store of some kind. Whether storage happens in table rows and columns, serialized as JSON strings, or as object graphs, we are still performing CRUD-based modeling. But this is not the only way to model the world. Instead of storing structures that model the state of our world, we can store events that lead to the current state of our world. This modeling approach is called event sourcing (*http://api.co/1TSQgo1*).

> Event sourcing is all about storing facts and any time you have "state" (structural models)—they are first-level derivative off of your facts. And they are transient.
>
> —Greg Young, Code on the Beach, 2014

In this context, by "facts" Young means the representative value of an event occurrence. An example could be "a package was transported from the last sorting facility, out for final delivery." Later in this chapter, we will see more examples of what facts can be.

It is fair to note that for the majority of software developers used to structural data modeling, event sourcing will initially sound alien and, maybe, even somewhat weird. But it really isn't. For one thing, event sourcing is not some bleeding-edge, untested theory dreamed up to solve problems in microservices. Event sourcing has been used in the financial industry with great success, independent of any microservice architecture association.

In addition, the roots and inspiration for event sourcing go way beyond microservices, the Internet itself, or even computers—all the way back to financial accounting and the paper-and-pen ledgers that contain a list of transactions, and never just the end value ("state") of a balance. Think of your bank account: there's a balance amount for your checking and savings accounts, but those are not first-class values that banks store in their databases. The account balance is always a derivative value; it's a function. More specifically, the balance is the sum of all transactions from the day you opened your account.

If you decide to dispute your current balance and call up your bank, they are not going to retort by saying, "But sir/ma'am, that's the value in our database, it has to be true!" Instead, they will print out all relevant transactions for you (or point you to online banking where you can do it yourself) and let you verify that the result of the transactions should indeed be equal to the balance value displayed. If you do find any errors with any of the transactions, the bank will issue a "compensating transaction" to fix the error. This is another crucial property of event sourcing: much like in life, we can never "go back" in time and "change" the past, we can only do something in the present to compensate for the mistakes of the past. In event sourcing, data is immutable—we always issue a new command/event to compensate rather than update a state of an entity, as we would do in a CRUD style.

When event sourcing is introduced to developers, the immediate concern is usually performance. If any state value is a function of events, we may assume that every access to the value would require recalculation of the current state from the source events. Obviously that would be extremely slow and generally unacceptable. Fortunately, in event sourcing, we can avoid such expensive operations by using a so-called rolling snapshot—a projection of the entity state at a given point in time. Depending on the event source implementation, it is common to snapshot intermediary values at various time points. For instance, you may precalculate your bank account balance on the last day of every month, so that if you need the balance on January 15, 2016 you will already have it on December 31, 2015 and will just need to calculate the projection for two weeks, instead of the entire life of the bank account. The specifics of how you implement rolling snapshots and projections may depend on the context of your application. Later in this chapter we will see that with a related pattern called CQRS, we can do much more than just cache states in rolling snapshots.

Despite its accounting roots, event sourcing is not only relevant to just financial use cases. For the rest of this chapter we will use a business scenario as far from banking and accounting as we could imagine: shipment and delivery of goods.

Remember the imaginary package-shipment startup Shipping, Inc. that we introduced in this chapter? As a parcel-delivery company, they need to accept packages, route them through various sorting warehouses (hops on the route), and eventually deliver to their destinations.

A representative data model for this system executed in structural style is shown in Figure 5-1.

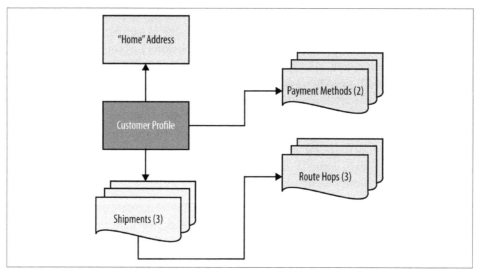

Figure 5-1. Data model for Shipping, Inc. using "current state" approach

The corresponding events-based model is shown in Figure 5-2.

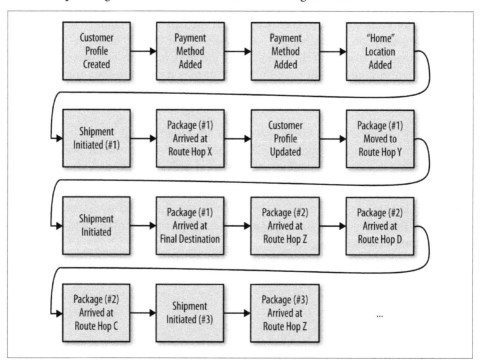

Figure 5-2. Data model for Shipping, Inc. using event sourcing

As you can see, the structural model strives to only save the current state of the system, while the event sourcing approach saves individual "facts." State, in event sourcing, is a function of all the pertinent facts that occurred. Not only does this give us full auditability (as demonstrated in the case when we called our bank to dispute the balance), we can also build state projections toward any time in the past, not just the "now." Would you like to know where all the packages were on Wednesday? No problem with event sourcing! Answering this question would be more difficult with the structural model, since it would require special coding.

If you enjoy noticing patterns in seemingly unrelated things the way we do, we urge you to take another look at the two diagrams. You may notice how every entity in the structural model is a "snowflake" (i.e., it has a unique "shape," in terms of properties and relationships, and was attentively crafted to represent differing real-life concepts). In contrast, events in an event store all look the same from the outside. This is a very similar view to another technology closely related to microservices: containers. Indeed, for the container host (e.g., a Docker (*https://www.docker.com/*) host), all containers look alike—the host doesn't "care" what is inside a container, it knows how to manage the lifecycle of a container independent of the contents of the container. In contrast, custom-installed enterprise applications have all kinds of peculiar "shapes" and environmental dependencies that the host must ensure exist (e.g., shared libraries the application expects). The "indifference to shape and contents" approach seems to be a trend in modern technologies, as we can see the same pattern in SQL versus NoSQL storage. It is very reminiscent, in its tendency to show up under multiple contexts, of the "batch-size reduction" trend we noticed earlier while looking at different modern methodologies across multiple disciplines (e.g., project management, product development, operations, and architecture). We love this—when the same pattern emerges in multiple places, we can use our understanding of the pattern to identify or predict "next big thing."

But let's get back to microservices. We dipped our toes in a data-modeling technology called event sourcing and noted some of its benefits compared to conventional, structural modeling, but how exactly does it help us solve the data isolation and encapsulation challenges of microservice architecture? As it turns out, we need one more design pattern, CQRS, to complement event sourcing and we will be well on our way toward being able to design effective data storage for microservices with data persistence models that can avoid data sharing at even very small microservice sizes.

System Model for Shipping, Inc.

As we noted earlier, a good start for a microservice system design is to identify bounded contexts in the system. Figure 5-3 shows a context map for key bounded contexts in our problem space. We will use this context map in discussing the solution throughout the chapter.

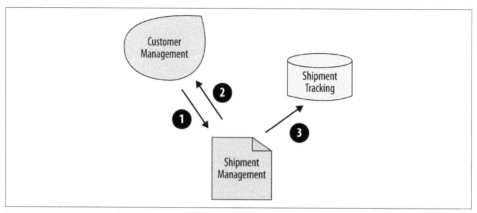

Figure 5-3. High-level context map for Shipping, Inc.'s microservice architecture

What are the capabilities of the three contexts and some of the data flows between the contexts, depicted by the arrows and numbers on the graph? They are as follows:

1. Customer Management creates, edits, enables/disables customer accounts, and can provide a representation of a customer to any interested context.

2. Shipment Management is responsible for the entire lifecycle of a package from drop-off to final delivery. It emits events as the package moves through sorting and forwarding facilities, along the delivery route.

3. Shipment Tracking is a reporting application that allows end users to track their shipments on their mobile device.

If we were to implement a data model of this application using a traditional, structural, CRUD-oriented model we would immediately run into data sharing and tight-coupling problems. Indeed, notice that the Shipment Management and Shipment Tracking contexts will have to query the same tables, at the very least the ones containing the transitions along the route. However, with event sourcing, the Shipment Management bounded context (and its corresponding microservice) can instead record events/commands and issue event notifications for other contexts and those other contexts will build their own data indexes (projections), never needing direct access to any data owned and managed by the Shipment Management microservice. The formal approach to this process is described in a pattern called CQRS.

CQRS

Command query responsibility segregation is a design pattern that states that we can (and sometimes should) separate data-update versus data-querying capabilities into separate models. It tracks its ancestry back to a principle called command–query separation (CQS), which was introduced by Bertrand Meyer in his book *Object-Oriented*

Software Construction (Prentice-Hall, 1997). Meyer argued that data-altering operations should be in different methods, separated from methods performing read-only operations. CQRS takes this concept a large step further, instructing us to use entirely different models for updates versus queries. This seemingly simple statement often turns out to be powerful enough to save the day, especially in the complicated case of the reports-centric microservices we mentioned earlier in this chapter.

Since reports usually need to aggregate and contrast data generated in different parts of a large system, they often need to span multiple subsystems and bounded contexts and almost always require access to data from multiple contexts. But it is only so if we assume we have a single model for any entity, where we both query and update the entity. If we instead use CQRS, the need to access data across multiple contexts (and related problems) can be eliminated. With CQRS, the Shipment Management microservice can "own" and encapsulate any updates related to package delivery, just notifying other contexts about events occurring. By subscribing to notifications of these events, a reporting service such as Shipment Tracking can build completely independent, query-optimized model(s) that don't need to be shared with any other service.

Figure 5-4 shows a conceptual diagram that depicts CQRS for our Shipping, Inc. application.

As you can see, thanks to CQRS, we were able to completely separate the data models of the Shipment Management and Tracking microservices. In fact, Shipping Management doesn't even need to know about the existence of the Tracking microservice, and the only thing the Tracking microservice relies on is a stream of events to build its query index. During runtime the Tracking microservice only queries its own index. Furthermore, the Tracking microservice can include event and command data from other microservices using the same flow, keeping its independence and loose coupling.

The big win with using event sourcing and CQRS is that they allow us to design very granular, loosely coupled components. With bounded contexts our boundaries have to align with business capabilities and subdomain boundaries. With event sourcing, we can literally create microservices so tiny that they just manage one type of event or run a single report. Targeted use of event sourcing and CQRS can take us to the next level of autonomous granularity in microservice architecture. As such, they play a crucial role in the architectural style.

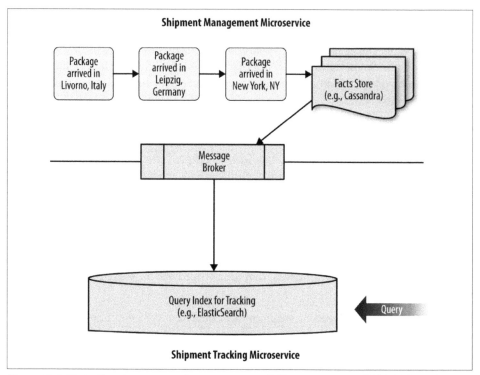

Figure 5-4. Data flow in command-query responsibility segregation (CQRS)-based model for Shipping, Inc.

Be careful not to abuse/overuse event sourcing and CQRS. You should only use event sourcing and CQRS when necessary, since they will complicate your implementation. Event sourcing and CQRS are not an "architecture" for your entire system, rather they are a powerful toolset to be used sparingly. There are still many use cases in which the conventional, CRUD-based model is much simpler and should be preferred.

Distributed Transactions and Sagas

The shared data model is not the only use case that can introduce tight coupling between microservices. Another important threat is workflows. A lot of real-life processes cannot be represented with a single, atomic operation, since they are a sequence of steps. When we are dealing with such workflows, the result only makes sense if all of the steps can be executed. In other words, if any step in the sequence fails, the resulting state of the relevant system becomes invalid. You probably recognize this problem from RDBMS systems where we call such processes "transactions." However, database transactions are local, contained within the confines of a single database where their implementations predominantly rely on the use of a shared state (i.e., we put locks on the rows and tables that participate in a transaction, guaranteeing data consistency). Once the transaction is fully executed we can remove the locks, or if any step of the transaction steps fails, we can roll back the steps already attempted.

For distributed workflows and share-nothing environments (and microservice architecture is both of those), we cannot use traditional transaction implementations with data locks and ACID compliance, since such transactions require shared data and local execution. Instead, an effective approach many teams use is known as "Sagas" (*ftp://ftp.cs.princeton.edu/reports/1987/070.pdf*). Sagas were designed for long-lived, distributed transactions by Hector Garcia-Molina and Kenneth Salem, and introduced in 1987 (yes, way before microservices or even the Web) during their work at Princeton University.

Sagas are very powerful because they allow running transaction-like, reversible workflows in distributed, loosely coupled environments without making any assumptions on the reliability of each component of the complex system or the overall system itself. The compromise here is that Sagas cannot always be rolled back to the exact initial state of the system before the transaction attempt. But we can make a best effort to bring the system to a state that is consistent with the initial state through compensation.

In Sagas, every step in the workflow executes its portion of the work, registers a callback to a "compensating transaction" in a message called a "routing slip," and passes the updated message down the activity chain. If any step downstream fails, that step looks at the routing slip and invokes the most recent step's compensating transaction, passing back the routing slip. The previous step does the same thing, calling its predecessor compensating transaction and so on until all already executed transactions are compensated.

Consider this example: let's say a customer mailed a prepaid cashier's check for $100 via Shipping, Inc.'s insured delivery. When the courier showed up at the destination, they found out that the address was wrong and the resident wouldn't accept the package. Thus, Shipping, Inc. wasn't able to complete the transaction. Since the package was insured, it is Shipping, Inc.'s responsibility to "roll back" the transaction and return the money to the sender. With ACID-compliant transactions, Shipping, Inc. is supposed to bring the exact $100 check back to the original sender, restoring the system state to its exact initial value. Unfortunately, on the way back the package was lost. Since Shipping, Inc. could no longer "roll back" the transaction, they decided to reimburse the insured value of $100 by depositing that amount into the customer's account. Since this was an active, long-time Shipping, Inc. customer and a rational human being, they didn't care which $100 was returned to them. The system didn't return to its exact initial state, but the compensating transaction brought the environment back to a consistent state. This is basically how Sagas work.

Due to its highly fault-tolerant, distributed nature, Sagas are very well-suited to replace traditional transactions when transactions across microservice boundaries are required in a microservice architecture. If you want to learn more about Sagas and see working code implementing a very expressive example related to travel booking, check out the Saga example (*http://api.co/1TSOxiI*) by Clemens Vasters.

Asynchronous Message-Passing and Microservices

Asynchronous message-passing plays a significant role in keeping things loosely coupled in a microservice architecture. You probably noticed that in one of the examples earlier in this chapter, we used a message broker to deliver event notifications from our Shipment Management microservice to the Shipment Tracking microservice in an asynchronous manner. That said, letting microservices directly interact with message brokers (such as RabbitMQ, etc.) is rarely a good idea. If two microservices are directly communicating via a message-queue channel, they are sharing a data space (the channel) and we have already talked, at length, about the evils of two microservices sharing a data space. Instead, what we can do is encapsulate message-passing behind an independent microservice that can provide message-passing *capability*, in a loosely coupled way, to all interested microservices.

The message-passing workflow we are most interested in, in the context of microservice architecture, is a simple publish/subscribe workflow. How do we express it as an HTTP API/microservice in a standard way? We recommend basing such a workflow on an existing standard, such as PubSubHubbub (*https://github.com/pubsubhubbub/PubSubHubbub*). Now to be fair, PubSubHubbub wasn't created for APIs or hypermedia APIs, it was created for RSS and Atom feeds in the blogging context. That said, we can adapt it relatively well to serve a hypermedia API-enabled workflow. To do so, we need to implement a flow similar to the one shown in Figure 5-5.

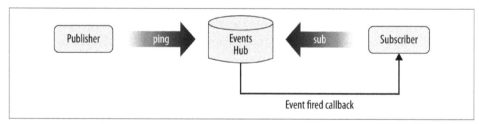

Figure 5-5. Asynchronous message-passing implemented with a PubSubHubbub-inspired flow

We also need to standardize some hypermedia affordances:

rel="hub"
> Refers to a hub that enables registration for notification of updates to the context.

rel="pingback"
> Gives the address of the pingback resource for the link context (*http://www.iana.org/assignments/link-relations/link-relations.xhtml*).

rel="sub"
> When included in a resource representation of an event, the "sub" (subscription) link relation *may* identify a target resource that represents the ability to subscribe to the pub/sub event-type resource in the link context.

rel="unsub"
> When included in a resource representation of an event, the "unsub" (subscription cancellation) link relation *may* identify a target resource that represents the ability to unsubscribe from the pub/sub event-type resource in the link context.

rel="event"
> Resource representation of a subscribable events.

rel="events"
> Link to a collection resource representing a list of subscribable events.

Dealing with Dependencies

Another important topic related to independent deployability is embedding of dependencies. Let's imagine that Shipping, Inc.'s currency rates microservice is being hammered by user queries and requests from other microservices. It would cost us much less if we hosted that microservice in a public cloud rather than on expensive servers of our corporate data center. But it doesn't seem possible to move the microservice to another host, if it stores data in the same SQL or NoSQL database system as all other microservices.

Please note that data tables are not shared, just the installation of the database-management system. It seems like the logical conclusion is that we cannot have any microservice share even the installation of a data storage system. Some may argue that a microservice needs to "embed" every single dependency it may require, so that the microservice can be deployed wherever and whenever, without any coordination with the rest of the system.

A strict requirement of full dependency embedding can be a significant problem, since for decades we have designed our architectures with centralized data storage, as shown in Figure 5-6.

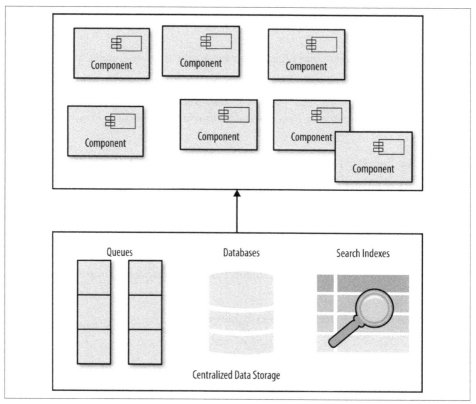

Figure 5-6. Components using a centralized pool of dependencies

Centralized data storage is operationally convenient: it allows dedicated, specialized teams (DBAs, sysadmins) to maintain and fine-tune these complex systems, obscuring the complexity from the developers.

In contrast, microservices favor *embedding of all their dependencies*, in order to achieve independent deployability. In such a scenario, every microservice manages and embeds its database, key-value store, search index, queue, etc. Then moving this microservice anywhere becomes trivial. This deployment would look like Figure 5-7.

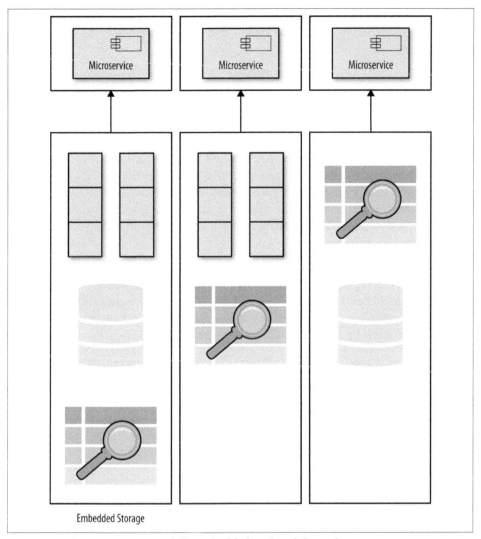

Figure 5-7. Components using fully embedded, isolated dependencies

The postulate of wholesale embedding of (data storage) dependencies looks beautiful on the surface, but in practice it is extremely wasteful for all but the simplest use cases. It is obvious that you will have a very hard time embedding entire Cassandra, Oracle, or ElasticSearch clusters in each and every microservice you develop. Especially if you are far down the microservices journey and possibly have hundreds of microservices. This is just not doable. Neither is it necessary.

In reality, a microservice doesn't have to carry along every single dependency (such as a data storage system) in order to be mobile and freely move across the data centers. Let us explain.

In his previous job, one of us (Irakli) traveled a lot for work. He'd acquired important tips for doing it efficiently—tips that he was completely indifferent to during his previous life as a casual traveler. As any frequent traveler will tell you, the most important rule for mobility is to keep your luggage light. You don't have to pack literally everything you may possibly need. For example, nobody packs shower-heads and towels on a business trip: you know you will find those at the hotel. If you know that the destination hotel has a convenience shop and your employer pays for incidentals, you don't even have to pack most toiletries. Irakli learned what he could count on being available "onsite" and what he needed to always bring with him. And, to pack light, he learned to limit his "dependencies" on a lot of things that were not needed as part of his packing routine.

Likewise, the trick to microservice mobility is not packing everything but instead ensuring that the deployment destination provides heavy assets, such as database clusters, in a usable and auto-discoverable form at every destination where a microservice may be deployed. Microservices should be written so that they can quickly discover those assets upon deployment and start using them.

 Let's be clear: data sharing between microservices is still the ultimate no-no. Sharing data creates tight coupling between microservices, which kills their mobility. However, sharing a database cluster installation is absolutely OK, given that each microservice only accesses isolated, namespaced portions of it.

Pragmatic Mobility

Figure 5-8 shows what a proper, sophisticated microservices deployment should look like in practice.

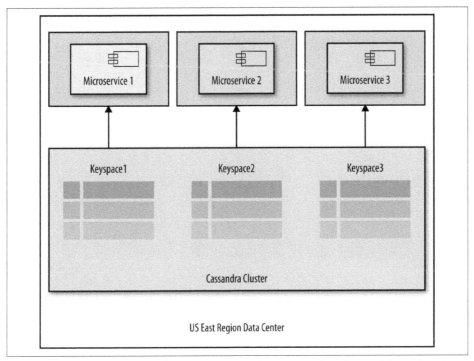

Figure 5-8. Pragmatic approach: Components using a centralized pool of dependencies, without sharing data spaces

If we decide to move Microservice 1 to another data center, it will expect that the new data center also has a functioning Cassandra cluster with a compatible version (in our earlier metaphor, the hotel provides towels we can use), but it will find a way to move its slice of data and won't depend on the existence or state of any other microservice at the destination (Figure 5-9).

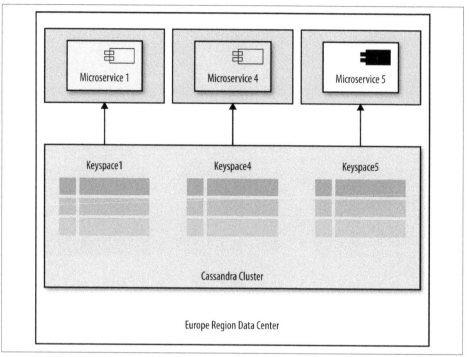

Figure 5-9. Pragmatic approach: Microservice 1's move to different data center made possible without data sharing

Microservices do not have to "travel" heavy and pack everything they may possibly require. In complicated cases it is OK to have some reasonable expectations about the destination environment, especially when it comes to complex data-storage capabilities.

The most important question we need to ask, when deciding on embedding dependencies versus "expecting" traits in an environment, is will our decision increase or decrease mobility? Our goal is to maximize deployment mobility of a microservice, which may mean different things in different contexts.

Summary

In this chapter we described a framework for effectively designing individual microservices and reviewed core modeling tools that a microservice architect needs to have in their toolbelt. We set out by demystifying the answer to one of the most commonly asked questions in microservices: how do we properly size services and identify boundaries? We started by clarifying the role of domain-driven design in the context of microservice architecture, the importance of bounded contexts, and gave an example of a context map for a fictional package delivery company Shipping, Inc.

We explained the overarching role of the "batch-size reduction" technique for systems engineering, when achieving both speed and safety at scale is the desired outcome. We demonstrated that at certain levels of granularity architects may require additional patterns, on top of the ones in domain-driven design, such as event sourcing, CQRS, and Sagas. We showed how these patterns can substantially alter our perspective on model design and how that can lead to more loosely coupled, splittable services.

Last, but not least, microservices are APIs, so going beyond code, implementation, and deployment considerations, we dedicated a significant portion of the chapter to explaining unique interface design needs for APIs that constitute a microservice.

CHAPTER 6

System Design and Operations

Having introduced a system-level view of the microservice architecture and architectural perspective of the value proposition, as well as design considerations, it's time to discuss aspects of runtime, operational management of a microservice architecture. The benefits of adopting a microservice architecture don't necessarily come free—they can shift complexity into operations. Generally speaking, teams adopting a microservice architecture are expected to have a certain level of infrastructure automation and operational maturity to be successful. Let's see what this means in practical terms.

In this chapter we will review key concepts of microservice operations such as independent deployability, the role of containers in cost-efficient deployments, and specifically, what role Docker can play in microservices, service discovery, security, routing, transformation, and orchestration. Taken together, discussions of these topics, in the context, will give you a solid foundation for understanding, designing, and executing on microservice architecture's operational needs.

Independent Deployability

One of the core principles of the microservice architectural style (*http://martin fowler.com/articles/microservices.html*) is the principle of independent deployability—i.e., each microservice must be deployable completely independent of any other microservice. Some of the most important benefits of the architectural style rely on faithful adherence to this principle.

Independent deployability allows us to perform selective or on-demand scaling; if a part of the system (e.g., a single microservice) experiences high load we can re-deploy or move that microservice to an environment with more resources, without having to scale up hardware capacity for the entire, typically large, enterprise system. For many organizations, the operational ability of selective scaling can save large amounts of money and provide essential flexibility.

Remember the imaginary package-shipment startup Shipping, Inc. we introduced in Chapter 5? As a parcel-delivery company, they need to accept packages, route them through various sorting warehouses (hops on the route), and eventually deliver them to their destinations.

Let's consider an example of selective scaling for Shipping, Inc. This company stores and operates sensitive customer information including demographic and financial data for its customers. In particular, Shipping, Inc. collects credit card information and, as such, falls under the auditing requirements of strict government regulation. For security reasons, Shipping, Inc. deploys sensitive parts of the implementation at an on-premise data center, but its CTO would still like to utilize "cloud computing," for cost and scalability reasons, when possible.

Scaling hardware resources on-premise can be extremely costly—we have to buy expensive hardware in *anticipation* of the usage rather than in response to actual usage. At the same time, the part of the application that gets hammered under load and needs scaling may not contain any sensitive client or financial data. It can be something as trivial as an API returning a list of US states or an API capable of converting various currency rates. The chief architect of Shipping, Inc. is confident that their security team will easily allow deployment of such safe microservices to a public/private cloud, where scaling of resources is significantly cheaper. The question is— could they deploy part of an application to a separate data center, a cloud-based one, in this case? The way most, typically monolithic, enterprise systems are architected, deploying selective parts of the application independently is either very hard or practically impossible. Microservices, in contrast, emphasize the requirement of independent deployability to the level of core principle, thus giving us much needed operational flexibility.

On top of operational cost saving and flexibility, another significant benefit of the independent deployability is an organizational one. Generally speaking, two different teams would be responsible for the development of separate microservices (e.g., Customer Management and Shipment Management). If the first team, which is responsible for the Customer Management microservice, needs to make a change and re-release, but Customer Management cannot be released independent of the Shipment Management microservice, we now need to coordinate Customer Management's release with the team that owns Shipment Management. Such coordination can be costly and complicated, since the latter team may have completely different priorities from the team responsible for Customer Management. More often than not the necessity of such coordination will delay a release. Now imagine that instead of just a handful we potentially have hundreds of microservices maintained by dozens of teams. Release coordination overhead can be devastating for such organizations, leading to products that ship with significant delays or sometimes get obsolete by the time they can be shipped. Eliminating costly cross-team coordination challenges is indeed a significant motivation for microservice adopters.

More Servers, More Servers! My Kingdom for a Server!

To ensure independent deployability, we need to develop, package, and release every microservice using an autonomous, isolated unit of environment. But what does "autonomous, isolated unit of environment" mean in this context? What are some examples of such units of environment?

Let's assume we are developing a Java/JEE application. At first glance, something like a WAR or EAR file may seem like an appropriate unit of encapsulation and isolation. After all, that's what these packaging formats were designed for—to distribute a collection of executable code and related resources that together form an independent application, within the context of an application server.

In reality, lightweight packaging solutions, such as JAR, WAR, and EAR archives in Java, Gem files (for Ruby), NPM modules (for Node), or PIP packages (for Python) don't provide sufficient modularity and the level of isolation required for microservices. WAR files and Gem files still share system resources like disk, memory, shared libraries, the operating system, etc. Case in point: a WAR or EAR file will typically expect a specific version of Java SDK and application server (JBoss, WebSphere, Weblogic, etc.) to be present in the environment. They may also expect specific versions of OS libraries in the environment. As any experienced sysadmin or DevOps engineer knows, one application's environmental expectations can be drastically different from another's, leading to version and dependency conflicts if we need to install both applications on the same server. One of the core motivations of adopting a microservice architecture is to avoid the need for complex coordination and conflict resolution, thus packaging solutions that are incapable of avoiding such interdependencies are not suitable for microservices. We need a higher level of component isolation to guarantee independent deployability.

What if we deployed a microservice per physical server or per virtual machine? Well, that would certainly meet the high bar of isolation demanded by microservices, but what would be the financial cost of such a solution?

For companies that have been using microservice architecture for a number of years, it is not uncommon to develop and maintain hundreds of microservices. Let's assume you are a mature microservices company with about 500 microservices. To deploy these microservices in a reliable, redundant manner you will need at least three servers/VMs per each microservice, resulting in 1,500 servers just for the production system. Typically, most companies run more than one environment (QA, stage, integration, etc.), which quickly multiplies the number of required servers.

Here comes the bad news: thousands of servers cost a lot. Even if we use VMs and not physical servers, even in the "cheapest" cloud-hosting environment the budget for a setup utilizing thousands of servers would be significantly high, probably higher than what most companies can afford or would like to spend. And then there's that important question of development environments. Most developers like to have a working, complete, if scaled down, model of the production environment on their workstations. How many VMs can we realistically launch on a single laptop or desktop computer? Maybe five or ten, at most? Definitely not hundreds or thousands.

So, what does this quick, on-a-napkin-style calculation of microservices hosting costs mean? Is a microservice architecture simply unrealistic and unattainable, from an operational perspective? It probably was, for most companies, some number of years ago. And that's why you see larger companies, such as Amazon and Netflix, being the pioneers of the architectural style—they were the few who could justify the costs. Things, however, have changed significantly in recent years.

Microservice Architecture is a Product of Its Time

We often get asked—what is the fundamental difference between microservice architecture and service-oriented architecture, especially given that so many underlying principles seem similar? We believe that the two architectural styles are creations of their respective eras, roughly a decade apart. In those 10 years we, as an industry, have gotten significantly more skilled in effective ways of automating infrastructure operations. Microservice architecture is leveraging the most advanced achievements in DevOps and continuous delivery, making the benefits of the architectural style available and cost-effective to much wider audiences than just a handful of large early adopters like Amazon or Netflix.

The reason microservice architecture is financially and operationally feasible has a lot to do with containers.

The deployment unit universally used for releasing and shipping microservices is a container. If you have never used containers before, you can think of a container as of an extremely lightweight "virtual machine." The technology is very different from that of conventional VMs. It is based on a Linux kernel extension (LXC) that allows running many isolated Linux environments (containers) on a single Linux host sharing the operating system kernel, which means we can run hundreds of containers on a single server or VM and still achieve the environment isolation and autonomy that is on par with running independent servers, and is therefore entirely acceptable for our microservices needs.

Containers will not be limited to just Linux in the future. Microsoft is actively working on supporting similar technology on the Windows platform (*http://api.co/1NZl5Hp*).

Containers provide a modern isolation solution with practically zero overhead. While we cannot run more than a handful of conventional VMs on a single host, it is completely possible to run hundreds of containers on a single host. Currently the most widely deployed container toolset is Docker, so in practice Docker and containers have become somewhat synonymous. In reality, there are other up-and-coming container solutions, which may gain more prominence in the future.

Docker and Microservices

In this section we discuss Docker as it is *the* container toolset most widely deployed in production today. However, as we already mentioned, alternative container solutions exist in varying stages of production readiness. Therefore, most things in this section should be understood as relevant to containers in general, not just Docker specifically.

At the beginning of 2016 (the time of writing of this book), most microservices deployments are practically unthinkable without utilizing Docker containers. We have discussed some of the practical reasons for this. That said, we shouldn't think of Docker or containers as tools designed just for the microservice architecture.

Containers in general, and Docker specifically, certainly exist outside microservice architecture. As a matter of fact, if we look at the current systems operations landscape we can see that the number of individuals and companies using containers many times exceeds those implementing microservice architecture. Docker in and of itself is significantly more common than the microservice architecture.

Containers were not created for microservices. They emerged as a powerful response to a practical need: technology teams needed a capable toolset for universal and predictable deployment of complex applications. Indeed, by packaging our application as a Docker container, which assumes prebundling all the required dependencies at the correct version numbers, we can enable others to reliably deploy it to any cloud or on-premise hosting facility, without worrying about target environment and compatibility. The only remaining deployment requirement is that the servers should be Docker-enabled—a pretty low bar, in most cases. In comparison, if we just gave somebody our application as an executable, without prebundled environmental dependencies we would be setting them up for a load of dependency pain. Alternatively if we wanted to package the same software as a VM image, we would have to create multiple VM images for several major platforms, since there is no single, dominant VM standard currently adopted by major players.

But compatibility is not the only win; there's another benefit that is equally, if not more, important when we consider containers versus VM images. Linux containers use a layered filesystem architecture known as union mounting. This allows a great extensibility and reusability not found in conventional VM architectures. With containers, it is trivial to extend your image from the "base image." If the base image updates, your container will inherit the changes at the next rebuild. Such a layered, inheritable build process promotes a collaborative development, multiplying the efforts of many teams. Centralized registries, discovery services, and community-oriented platforms such as Docker Hub and GitHub further facilitate quick adoption and education in the space.

As a matter of fact, we could easily turn the tables and claim that it is Docker that will be driving the adoption of microservices instead of vice versa. One of the reasons for this claim is that Docker puts significant emphasis on the "Unix philosophy" of shipping containers, i.e., "do one thing, and do it well." Indeed, this core principle is prominently outlined in the Docker documentation itself (*http://api.co/1THnJyq*):

> Run only one process per container. In almost all cases, you should only run a single process in a single container. Decoupling applications into multiple containers makes it much easier to scale horizontally and reuse containers.
>
> —Docker documentation

It is clear that with such principles at its core Docker philosophy is much closer to the microservice architecture than a conventional, large monolithic architecture. When you are shooting for "doing one thing" it makes little sense to containerize your entire, huge, enterprise application as a single Docker container. Most certainly you would want to first modularize the application into loosely coupled components that communicate via standard network protocols, which, in essence, is what the microservice architecture delivers. As such, if you start with a goal of containerizing your large and complex application you will likely need a certain level of microservice design in your complex application.

The way we like to look at it, Docker containers and microservice architecture are two ends of the road that lead to the same ultimate goal of continuous delivery and operational efficiency. You may start at either end, as long as the desired goals are achieved.

If you are new to Docker and would like a quick sneak peek at Docker for microservices, you can find one in a blog post Irakli recently published (*http://api.co/1TOgeLb*).

The Role of Service Discovery

If you are using Docker containers to package and deploy your microservices, you can use a simple Docker Compose configuration to orchestrate multiple microservices (and their containers) into a coherent application. As long as you are on a single host (server) this configuration will allow multiple microservices to "discover" and communicate with each other. This approach is commonly used in local development and for quick prototyping.

But in production environments, things can get significantly more complicated. Due to reliability and redundancy needs, it is very unlikely that you will be using just one Docker host in production. Instead, you will probably deploy at least three or more Docker hosts, with a number of containers on each one of them.

Furthermore, if your services get significantly different levels of load, you may decide to not deploy all services on all hosts but end up deploying high-load services on a select number of hosts (let's say ten of them), while low-load services may only be deployed on three servers, and not necessarily the same ones. Additionally, there may be security- and business-related reasons that may cause you to deploy some services on certain hosts and other services on different ones.

In general, how you distribute your services across your available hosts will depend on your business and technical needs and very likely may change over time. Hosts are just servers, they are not guaranteed to last forever.

Figure 6-1 shows what the nonuniform distribution of your services may look like at some point in time if you have four hosts with four containers.

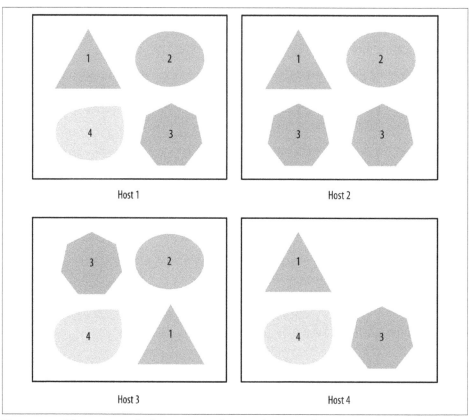

Figure 6-1. Microservice deployment topology with nonuniform service distribution

Each instance of the microservice container in Figure 6-1 is depicted with a different number, shape, and color. In this example, we have Microservice 1 deployed on all four hosts, but Microservice 2 is only on hosts 1–3. Keep in mind that the deployment topology may change at any time, based on load, business rules, which host is available, and whether an instance of your microservice suddenly crashes or not.

Note that since typically many services are deployed on the same host, we cannot address a microservice by just an IP address. There are usually too many microservices, and the instances of those can go up and down at any time. If we allocated an IP per microservice, the IP address allocation + assignment would become too complicated. Instead, we allocate an IP per host (server) and the microservice is fully addressed with a combination of:

1. IP address (of the host)
2. Port number(s) the service is available at on the host

We already noted that the IPs a microservice is available at are ever-changing, but what about the port? You might assume that we can assign fixed ports to individual microservices, in essence saying, "our account management microservice always launches on port 5555." But this would not be a good idea. Generally speaking, many different teams will need to independently launch microservices on, likely, a shared pool of hosts. If we assumed that a specific microservice always launches on a specific port of a host, we would require a high level of cross-team coordination to ensure that multiple teams don't accidentally claim the same port. But one of the main motivations of using a microservice architecture is eliminating the need for costly cross-team coordination. Such coordination is untenable, in general. It is also unnecessary since there are better ways to achieve the same goal.

This is where service discovery enters the microservices scene. We need some system that will keep an eye on all services at all times and keep track of which service is deployed on which IP/port combination at any given time, so that the clients of microservices can be seamlessly routed accordingly.

As mentioned in previous chapters, there are several established solutions in the open source space for service discovery. On one side of the spectrum we have tools such as Etcd from CoreOs and Consul by HashiCorp. They are "low-level" tools providing a high degree of control and visibility to an architect. On the other side of the spectrum are tools that provide "container-scheduling" capabilities, alongside the service discovery. Kubernetes from Google is probably the most well-known in this category, Docker Swarm being another, more recent player. With container-scheduling solutions, we get a high degree of automation and abstraction. In this scenario, instead of deciding which container is launched on which servers, we just tell the system how much of the host pool's resources should be devoted to a particular service and Kubernetes or Swarm takes care of balancing/rebalancing containers on the hosts, based on these criteria. Another important technology utilizing containers is Mesosphere. Mesosphere is even more abstracted than Kubernetes or Swarm, currently marketed as "a data center operating system" that allows a higher degree of automation, without having to worry about the many nodes deployed, and operating the entire server cluster almost as if it were a single superserver.

There are no "better" tools when considering service discovery. As an architect, we need to decide how much automation "magic" we want from our tools versus how much control we need to retain for ourselves. Even within the same enterprise application, it is very likely that you may find Kubernetes a great fit for a certain batch of microservices, whereas architects may decide that another class of microservices can be better deployed if directly managed using something like Consul.

The Need for an API Gateway

A common pattern observed in virtually all microservice implementations is teams securing API endpoints, provided by microservices, with an API gateway. Modern API gateways provide an additional, critical feature required by microservices: transformation and orchestration. Last but not least, in most mature implementations, API gateways cooperate with service discovery tools to route requests from the clients of microservices. In this section of the chapter, we will look into each one of the API gateway features and clarify their role in the overall architecture of the operations layer for microservices.

Security

Microservice architecture is an architecture with a significantly high degree of freedom. Or in other words, there are a lot more moving parts than in a monolithic application. As we mentioned earlier, in mature microservices organizations where the architecture is implemented for complex enterprise applications, it is common to have hundreds of microservices deployed. Things can go horribly wrong security-wise when there are many moving parts. We certainly need some law and order to keep everything in control and safe. Which is why, in virtually all microservice implementations, we see API endpoints provided by various microservices secured using a capable API gateway.

APIs provided by microservices may call each other, may be called by "frontend," i.e., public-facing APIs, or they may be directly called by API clients such as mobile applications, web applications, and partner systems. Depending on the microservice itself, the business needs of the organization, and the industry, market, or application context—all scenarios are fair game. To make sure we never compromise the security of the overall system, the widely recommended approach is to secure invocation of "public-facing" API endpoints of the microservices-enabled system using a capable API gateway.

Based on our experience building microservices systems and helping a wide variety of organizations do the same, we recommend a more radical approach than just securing "public API endpoints."

In reality the distinction between "public" and "private" APIs often ends up being arbitrary. How certain are we that the API we think is "only internal" will never be required by any outside system? As soon as we try to use an API over the public Web, from our own web application or from a mobile application, as far as security is concerned, that endpoint is "public" and needs to be secured. We have mentioned Amazon multiple times in this book. Let's remember what the big picture was for Amazon, with Amazon Web Services: they in essence exposed the lowest level of the technical stack possible—hardware resources such as disk, CPU, networking etc., used by their ecommerce website—for anybody in the world to use and they made billions out of it. So, why would we ever assume that we have some APIs that will forever be "internal only"?

Sometimes, certain microservices are deemed "internal" and excluded from the security provided by an API Gateway, as we assume that they can never be reached by external clients. This is dangerous since the assumption may, over time, become invalid. It's better to always secure any API/microservice access with an API gateway. In most cases the negligible overhead of introducing an API gateway in between service calls is well worth the benefits.

Transformation and Orchestration

We have already mentioned that microservices are typically designed to provide a single capability. They are the Web's version of embracing the Unix philosophy of "do one thing, and do it well." However, as any Unix developer will tell you, the single-responsibility approach only works because Unix facilitates advanced *orchestration* of its highly specialized utilities, through universal piping of inputs and outputs. Using pipes, you can easily combine and chain Unix utilities to solve nontrivial problems involving sophisticated process workflows. A critical need for a similar solution exists in the space of APIs and microservices as well. Basically, to make microservices useful, we need an orchestration framework like Unix piping, but one geared to web APIs.

Microservices, due to their narrow specialization and typically small size, are very useful deployment units for the teams producing them. That said, they may or may not be as convenient for consumption, depending on the client. The Web is a distributed system. Due to its distributed nature, on the Web, so-called "chatty" interfaces are shunned. Those are interfaces where you need to make many calls to get the data required for a single task. This distaste for chatty interfaces is especially pronounced among mobile developers, since they often have to deal with unreliable, intermittent, and slow connections. There are a few things a mobile developer loathes more than an API interface that forces them to make multiple calls to retrieve something they consider a single piece of information.

Let's imagine that after successful completion of the APIs required for the mobile application, the technical team behind Shipping, Inc.'s microservice architecture decided to embark on a new journey of developing an "intelligent" inventory management system. The purpose of the new system is to analyze properly anonymized data about millions of shipments passing through Shipping, Inc., combine this insight with all of the metadata that is available on the goods being shipped, determine behavioral patterns of the consumers, and utilizing human + machine algorithms design a "recommendation engine" capable of suggesting optimal inventory levels to Shipping, Inc.'s "platinum" customers. If everything works, those suggestions will be able to help customers achieve unparalleled efficiency in managing product stock, addressing one of the main concerns of any online retailer.

If the team is building this system using a microservice architecture, they could end up creating two microservices for the main functionality:

1. Recommendations microservice, which takes user information in, and responds with the list containing the recommendations—i.e., suggested stock levels for various products that this customer typically ships.

2. Product Metadata microservice, which takes in an ID of a product type and retrieves all kinds of useful metadata about it.

Such separation of concerns, into specialized microservices, makes complete sense from the perspective of the API publisher, or as we may call them, the server-side team. However, for the team that is actually implementing the end-user interface, calling the preceding microservices is nothing but a headache. More likely than not, the mobile team is working on a user screen where they are trying to display several upcoming suggestions. Let's say the page size is 20, so 20 suggestions at a time. With the current, verbatim design of the microservices, the user-interface team will have to make 21 HTTP calls: one to retrieve the recommendations list and then one for each recommendation to retrieve the details, such as product name, dimensions, size, price, etc.

At this point, the user-interface team is not happy. They wanted a single list; but instead are forced to make multiple calls (the infamous "N+1 queries" problem (*http://api.co/1U7ZHw5*), resurfaced in APIs). Additionally, the calls to the Product Metadata microservice return too much information (large payload problem), which is an issue for, say, mobile devices on slow connections. And the end result is that the rendering of the all-important mobile screen is slow and sluggish, leading to poor user experience.

Scenarios like the one just described are all too common. As a matter of fact, they existed even before the dawn of the microservice architecture. For instance, the REST API style has been criticized a lot for "chatty interface." We do *not* have to build our microservice APIs in the RESTful style, but a similar problem still exists, since we decided that our microservices need to do "one thing," which can lead to chattiness. Fortunately, since the "chattiness" problem in the APIs is not new, mature API gateways are perfectly equipped to deal with the problem. A capable API gateway will allow you to declaratively, through configuration, create API interfaces that can orchestrate backend microservices and "hide" their granularity behind a much more developer-friendly interface and eliminate chattiness. In our example scenario, we can quickly aggregate the N+1 calls into a single API call and optimize the response payload. This gives mobile developers exactly what they need: a list of recommendations via a single query, with exactly the metadata they required. The calls to backend microservices will be made by the API gateway. Good API gateways can also parallelize the twenty calls to the Product Metadata microservice, making the aggregate call very fast and efficient.

Routing

We already mentioned that in order to properly discover microservices we need to use a service discovery system. Service discovery systems such as Consul and etcd will monitor your microservice instances and track metadata about what IPs and ports each one of your microservices is available at, at any given time. However, directly providing tuples of the IP/port combinations to route an API client is not an adequate solution. A proper solution needs to abstract implementation details from the client. An API client still expects to retrieve an API at a specific URI, regardless of whether there's a microservice architecture behind it and independent of how many servers, Docker containers, or anything else is serving the request.

Some of the service discovery solutions (e.g., Consul, and etcd using SkyDNS (*https:// github.com/skynetservices/skydns*)) provide a DNS-based interface to discovery. This can be very useful for debugging, but still falls short of production needs because normal DNS queries only look up domain/IP mapping, whereas for microservices we need domain mapping with an IP+port combination. In both Consul and SkyDNS, you can actually use DNS to look up both IP and port number, via an RFC 2782 SRV query (*https://www.consul.io/docs/agent/dns.html*), but realistically no API client expects or will appreciate having to make SRV requests before calling your API. This is not the norm. Instead, what we should do is let an API gateway hide the complexities of routing to a microservice from the client apps. An API gateway can interface with either HTTP or DNS interfaces of a service discovery system and route an API client to the correct service when an external URI associated with the microservice is requested. You can also use a load balancer or smart-reverse proxy to achieve the same goal, but since we already use API gateways to secure routes to microservices, it makes a lot of sense for the routing requirement to also be implemented on the gateway.

Monitoring and Alerting

As we have already mentioned, while microservice architecture delivers significant benefits, it is also a system with a lot more moving parts than the alternative—monolith. As such, when implementing a microservice architecture, it becomes very important to have extensive system-wide monitoring and to avoid cascading failures.

The same tools that we mentioned for service discovery can also provide powerful monitoring and failover capabilities. Let's take Consul as an example. Not only does Consul know how many active containers exist for a specific service, marking a service broken if that number is zero, but Consul also allows us to deploy customized health-check monitors for any service. This can be very useful. Indeed, just because a container instance for a microservice is up and running doesn't always mean the microservice itself is healthy. We may want to additionally check that the microservice is responding on a specific port or a specific URL, possibly even checking that the health ping returns predetermined response data.

In addition to the "pull" workflow in which Consul agents query a service, we can also configure "push"-oriented health checks, where the microservice itself is responsible for periodically checking in, i.e., push predetermined payload to Consul. If Consul doesn't receive such a "check-in," the instance of the service will be marked "broken." This alternative workflow is very valuable for scheduled services that must run on predetermined schedules. It is often hard to verify that scheduled jobs do run as expected, but the "push"-based health-check workflow can give us exactly what we need.

Once we set up health checks we can install an open source plug-in called Consul Alerts (*https://github.com/AcalephStorage/consul-alerts*), which can send service failure and recovery notifications to incident management services such as PagerDuty (*https://www.pagerduty.com/*) or OpsGenie (*https://www.opsgenie.com/*). These are powerful services that allow you to set up sophisticated incident-notification phone trees and/or notify your tech team via email, SMS, and push notifications through their mobile apps. Since it is 2016 and everybody seems to be using Slack (*https://slack.com/*) or HipChat (*https://www.hipchat.com/*), Consul Alerts also has support for notifying these chat/communication systems, so that you can be alerted about a service interruption even as you are sending your coworkers that day's funny animated *.gif*, or are, say, discussing product priorities for the upcoming cycle. I personally use Slack for both, so no judging.

Summary

In this chapter we clarified the relationship between containers (such as Docker) and microservices. While simply containerizing your application doesn't lead you to a microservice architecture, most microservices implementations do use containers as they bring unparalleled cost savings and portability for autonomous deployment. Further, we noted that containers were not created for microservices—they have their own purpose and are actually much more widely adopted than microservice architecture. We also predicted that container adoption may, in effect, lead to increased popularity of microservices, since it is the architecture that best fits the container-based deployment philosophy.

We also reviewed what is possibly the most important topic of microservices operations—service discovery—explaining the various options currently available in open source, the similarities and differences between them, and what choices systems architects make when picking a particular solution.

We discussed the role of the API gateway and the core capabilities it provides for the architectural style: security, routing, and transformation/orchestration. We also looked at an example of an intelligent recommendation engine to explain the key role of transformation/orchestration in the architectural style.

At the end of the chapter we discussed the role of monitoring for microservice architecture, alternative workflow approaches of push-based health-checks versus pull-based ones, and provided some example tools that can help teams set up sophisticated monitoring and alerting workflows.

CHAPTER 7

Adopting Microservices in Practice

Throughout this book we've talked about companies that have enjoyed success with the microservices style. In fact, a lot of the organizations that we've used to highlight the microservice architecture are the same ones that pop up in most of the online literature: Amazon, Netflix, and SoundCloud, among others. But chances are that your business doesn't look or act like one of these online companies. That's not a bad thing.

Doing things in the microservices way can apply to almost any organization. We believe that every organization that does business on the Internet has an opportunity to improve with a focus on balancing safety and speed at scale. From this focus, you can identify the principles and practices from our showcase microservices organizations that will work for you.

We also know that most readers are already working in a company with active IT services up and running in production. That means you're likely dealing with an existing legacy of culture, organizational structure, process, tools, services, and architecture. You're not going to be designing an optimized microservice-centric system from scratch. To adopt the microservices way of building applications, you'll need a set of principles and practices that fit your unique set of constraints and coax the system toward an optimal balance of safety and speed.

In this chapter we will highlight some of the most common adoption challenges that you will face when implementing a microservice-style architecture within an existing organization. These are arranged in a kind of question-and-answer format to help you zero in on the ones that interest you right now. While it isn't an exhaustive list, we hope it will help you tackle some of the biggest problems that mid- to large-sized companies have when wrestling with a microservices implementation. Hopefully, you'll be able to refer back to these topics several times as you work through your own microservice progress.

Solution Architecture Guidance

Solution architecture is distinct from individual service design elements because it represents a macro view of our solution. Here are some issues you may encounter when working at this macro-level view of the system.

How many bug fixes/features should be included in a single release?

Since releases are expected to happen frequently, each release will likely be small. You probably can't box up 50 changes to a single service component in a week. We hear most organizations have a practice of limiting the number of changes. Netflix, for example, tells teams to make only one significant change per release. For example, if your team needs to refactor some of the internal code *and* start using a new data store module, that would be two releases.

The biggest reason for limiting the number of changes in a release is to reduce uncertainty. If you release a component that contains multiple changes, the uncertainty is increased by the number of interactions that occur between those changes. The mathematical discipline of graph theory provides a simple formula to calculate those interactions: $n(n-1)/2$. Based on this, if you release a component that contains 5 changes and it causes problems in production, you know that there are 10 possible ways in which these 5 changes could interact to cause a problem. But if you release a component with 15 changes there is a potential for over 100 different ways in which those changes can interact to cause problems—and that's just internal problems.

Limit the number of changes in each release to increase the safety of each release.

When do I know our microservice transformation is done?

Technically, creating and maintaining a vital information system is never "done." And that is also true for one built in the microservices way. In our experience some architects and developers spend a lot of time trying to identify the ideal solution or implementation model for their system design. It rarely works. In fact, one of the advantages of microservices is that change over time is not as costly or dangerous as it might be in tightly coupled large-scope release models.

Trying to perfect "the system" is an impossible task since it will always be a moving target. Often arriving at some "final state" marks the start of accumulating "technical debt"—that status where the system is outdated and difficult to change. It helps to remember that everything you build today will likely be obsolete within a few years anyway.

Since doing things in the microservices way means lots of small releases over time, you'll always be changing/improving something. This means you get lots of "done" moments along the way and, in keeping with the theme of microservices, are able to effect change over time "at scale."

Organizational Guidance

From a microservice system perspective, organizational design includes the structure, direction of authority, granularity, and composition of teams. A good microservice system designer understands the implications of changing these organizational properties and knows that good service design is a byproduct of good organizational design.

How do I know if my organization is ready for microservices?

You can start by assessing your organization's structure and associated culture. In a 1967 paper titled "How Committees Invent" (*http://www.melconway.com/Home/ Conways_Law.html*), computer scientist Mel Conway argued that the design of a software system will mimic the communication structure of the organization that produced it. "Conway's law," as it came to be known, has had a recent revival in microservices circles. There is good reason for this. As discussed earlier, the majority of microservice architecture pioneers began their quest for faster software delivery by optimizing organizational design before addressing the software architecture. Given this progression, these organizations landed on microservice architecture as a style that aligned with their small, business-aligned teams, thus revealing the wisdom of Conway's decades-old assertion.

However, many organizations now evaluating microservice architecture are not following the same path. In those cases, it is crucial to look at the organizational structure. How are responsibilities divided between teams? Are they aligned to business domains, or technology skillsets? At what level of the organization are development and operations divided? How big are the teams? What skills do they have? How dynamic is the communication and interaction between the teams who need to be involved in the delivery lifecycle? In addition to these organizational variables, you should evaluate the culture. How is power distributed between the teams? Is it centralized at a high level, or decentralized among the delivery teams? Answering these questions will help you understand what impacts these organizational factors will have on your adoption efforts and resulting successes.

Assessing Your Organization

- How are responsibilities divided?
- Are responsibilities aligned to business or technology?
- Do you practice DevOps, or Dev and Ops?
- How big are the teams? What kinds of skills do they have?
- What are the dependencies for cross-team communication?
- What does the power distribution look like between teams?

The ideal organization for microservices has small, empowered teams responsible for services that align with specific business domains. These teams feature all of the roles necessary to deliver these services, such as product owners, architects, developers, quality engineers, and operational engineers. The teams also need the right skills, such as API design and development, and knowledge of distributed applications. Organizations that mismatch any of these characteristics will pay a toll when attempting to apply microservice architecture. Teams that are not empowered will experience delays waiting for decisions to be made above their heads. Lack of business alignment will lead to cross-team dependencies, causing further delays and architectural deviation. Teams that are too large create incomprehensible code bases that impede and delay future changes. The higher up the divide between development and operations, the less motivated the operations group will be to automate and optimize and the less diligent developers will be in the operability of their software. Lastly, if the team doesn't have the right skills to build API-fronted services using distributed concepts, costs could go up to cover training and/or contract hiring, or the solution could be dragged away from the microservices approach as existing resources retreat to their technological comfort zones.

Culture Guidance

Your organization's culture is important because it shapes all of the atomic decisions that people within the system will make. This large scope of influence is what makes it such a powerful tool in your system design endeavor.

How do I introduce change?

> ...the challenge is to find small changes that can unfold in a way that creates large effects...
>
> —Gareth Morgan, author of *Images of Organization*

If you aren't working in a *greenfield* environment, chances are you'll have inherited an existing organizational design as well. Making changes to a working organization is nontrivial and carries a much greater risk than toying with a solution architecture. After all, if we make a mistake when refactoring our software we can always undo our changes, but when we make a mistake when redesigning the reporting structure in an organization the damage is not so easily undone.

You're unlikely to hear anyone refer to organizational design using the term refactoring. You're far more likely to hear the term *organizational transformation*, and if it's an area of interest to you, there is a wealth of material that can help you along the path to change. But within the context of this book, the term refactoring makes a lot of sense. What we are primarily interested in is a method for making changes to the organization in a way that is *safe*. Refactoring can help us with that.

In order to apply a refactoring strategy to the organizational design, you'll need to:

1. Devise a way to test changes
2. Identify problem areas in your organizational design
3. Identify safe transformations (changes that don't change existing behavior)

Refactoring the organization won't help you do something you don't already know how to do. Your goal should be to do the same things, but improve the design of your organization so you can do them better.

When you refactor an application you can measure and observe the performance of the application; you can audit the source code, and you can comb through logs and determine where most of the problems occur. But when dealing with the processes and people that make up an organization things are a bit less black and white. To successfully identify where the refactoring opportunities are within the organization, you'll need to find some way to model the existing system in order to analyze and measure its performance.

SoundCloud's Phil Calçado has written about using a lean management technique called *value stream mapping* as an initial step toward microservices. Value stream maps are a great tool to use for this activity, but use whichever method you are comfortable with to get a better understanding of how work is being done. Flowcharts, business process models, and activity diagrams can all do the job in the right hands.

No matter how you do it, the goal in this step is to identify how software changes are introduced to the system, who implements those changes, and the type of coordination that is required for those changes to take place. For the microservice system we are especially interested in identifying opportunities to improve the efficiency of change. Gaining a total understanding of how your organization works may be too large of an initial investment to undertake, so in practice you may need to focus only on the changes that occur the most often for the components that are the most volatile.

In particular, you should be looking for the bottlenecks that cause change to be expensive. Which processes result in a queue or backlog? Are there particular centralized functions such as audits, code reviews, and gating procedures that cause teams to have to wait? Are there any parts of your process flow that make it difficult for multiple changes to be introduced at the same time due to resource availability or a need for serialized process execution? Finding these bottlenecks will help you identify good candidates for process and organizational refactoring as they should yield a large benefit to the changeability and speed of release for the system.

Can I do microservices in a project-centric culture?

A hallmark of a microservices organization is that the teams that implement a feature, application, or service continue to support, improve, and work on the code for its lifetime. This product-centric perspective instills a sense of ownership of the component and reinforces the idea that deployed components will constantly be updated and replaced. This notion of ownership is important enough that Martin Fowler has made "products not projects" (*http://martinfowler.com/articles/microservices.html*) one of the primary characteristics for a microservice application.

Typical project-centric cultures operate differently. Teams are formed to address a particular problem (e.g., create a new component, add a feature, etc.) and disbanded when that problem is solved. Often a good deal of knowledge about both the problem and the solution gets lost when the team disbands. And, if there is a need to re-address the same problem, or make additional changes to the same component, it may be difficult to re-create the team or recover the lost knowledge. These challenges usually mean changes happen less often and are more likely to result in bugs or partial solutions.

In truth, it is quite difficult to adopt the microservice style if you need to operate in this type of culture. If changeability and speed of release are important properties for your system, the long-term goal should be to transition to a style of building that encourages team-based ownership of components.

Can I do microservices with outsourced workers?

A particular challenge for large companies trying to incorporate the ideal microservices system is the trend toward outsourcing technology services. The act of hiring an outside company to perform development and operations activities using workers who are external to the organization seems at odds with the culture and organizational principles we've described in this book. But with the right outsourcing structure, a microservice system may lend itself well to being developed by an external organization.

By embracing a decentralized way of working and standardizing on the output and processes of service teams (containers and APIs), the outsourced development team can be given enough autonomy to build a service that meets the capability requirements of the owning organization. But this is only possible if the outsourced team conforms to the principles that exemplify the microservices way: the teams should be the *right* size, built to last for the perpetuity of the life of the service, and composed of workers who are skilled, experienced, and capable enough to make good design and implementation decisions autonomously.

In addition to team composition, the microservice designer should acknowledge that a cross-pollination of cultures occurs whenever outsourcing is conducted. The implication is that a desired organizational culture cannot simply be adopted by the outsourced team, nor can the buying organization avoid having their culture changed by the intermingling of work. This means that culture becomes an important element in deciding which companies or people should be chosen to support the outsourcing model.

Ultimately, the selection process for a microservices outsourcing model cannot be optimized purely for low-cost work. You will need to carefully select a partner who is amenable to the cultural traits you are looking for and possesses aspects of culture you'd like to incorporate into your own system. The deal must also be structured to incentivize the team dynamic that works best for building applications the microservices way—teams should be dedicated to services, workers should be capable of working autonomously, and speed of high-quality delivery should be the primary metric for success.

Tools and Process Guidance

The system behavior is also a result of the processes and tools that workers in the system use to do their job. In microservices systems, this usually includes tooling and processes related to software development, code deployment, maintenance, and product management.

What kinds of tools and technology are required for microservices?

Chapter 4 introduced the importance of the microservices platform and Chapters 5-6 identified some particularly important tools that you can use to "power up" your platform and maximize both speed and safety of change. But these aren't the only tools you'll need if you want to improve your chances of succeeding with microservices.

The ideal technological environment for microservices features cloud infrastructure, which facilitates rapid provisioning and automated deployment. The use of containers is particularly useful to enable portability and heterogeneity. Middleware for data storage, integration, security, and operations should be web API-friendly in order to facilitate automation and discovery, and should also be amenable to dynamic, decentralized distribution. The ideal programming languages for microservices are API friendly as well, and should be functional while also matching the skillsets of your organization. It is particularly useful to provide tools for developers that simplify their tasks yet incorporate constraints that encourage good operational behavior of their resulting code.

Straying from these technological traits can lead to adoption issues. Lack of cloud infrastructure will lead to deployment delays and inflexible scaling. Lack of containers—or reliance on older virtualization or app servers—could increase the cost of resource utilization and lead to quality issues resulting from inconsistencies across environments. Middleware that assumes strict centralized control will break the decentralized organizational model and challenge the provisioning of ephemeral environments. If used in a decentralized model, this specialized middleware could also lead to skill challenges in the organization if every team is required to cultivate expertise. Centralized or segregated data breaks the organizational model as well. It also slows down delivery and impedes evolvability. Lack of developer tooling consistency could lead to duplicate work and lack of visibility or resiliency in the overall system. Finally, a large dependency on legacy applications could limit the ability to make changes.

What kinds of practices and processes will I need to support microservices?

While we talked about the principles that underpin good microservices practices in Chapter 4, we haven't told you which specific practices or methodologies you should use. Our advice is to focus on the principles first, but it's worth taking a look at how the companies that are known for doing microservices well build their software.

The ideal software development lifecycle for microservices is based on a product mentality using Agile principles (*http://agilemanifesto.org/principles.html*), which includes continuous integration and continuous delivery and features a high degree of automation in testing, deployment, and operations. Attempting to apply microservice architecture in a differing environment can subtract from its potential value. A Waterfall approach can lead to tight coupling of services, making it difficult to manage the different change rates of those services and inhibiting their evolution. Project-focused delivery assumes static requirements and heavyweight change control, both impediments to fast software delivery. Being unable to deploy frequently will lead to a "big bang" release mentality and bring with it undue ceremony. If change frequency is increased in an environment that has a legacy of change intolerance, many of those overweight processes can stick around, slowing down delivery, and introducing procedural fatigue as a new risk. Lack of automation in the deployment lifecycle will have a negative compound effect on speed to market, and lack of automation in operations will make it harder to deal with the operational complexity of a distributed environment.

How do I govern a microservice system?

Aside from regulatory issues (e.g., certification, audits, etc.) there are typically three ways in which you can address security and governance requirements in a microservice system: centralized, contextual, and decentralized.

Centralized controls

At the component level, there really isn't anything special about securing a microservice system. If you know how to secure an operating system, secure an API, or secure an application you can apply all of the same mechanisms to a microservice system. But when security mechanisms are introduced in the manner that most experts are used to implementing them, you can inadvertently upset the system optimization goals that you've worked hard to design into the architecture.

This is because security, controls, and governance policies are often implemented in a centralized fashion. For example, if we have a need to authenticate, authorize, and audit messages before they are processed, the most common architecture pattern is to implement some form of central security enforcement component within the architecture. Implementing a single, scalable component that can manage a complex and expensive function like access control makes a lot of sense. Assigning a separate team to manage and implement such a service also makes a lot of sense. Unfortunately, services like access control are likely to be used by every service in the infrastructure, which results in a common component that all of other services will grow dependent on. In other words, a bottleneck can develop.

A centralized security component risks putting our system into a state of *mechanical organization* or centralized control. In the early days of a microservice architecture it will be easy to set up the correct access and routing rules for a handful of services, but as more services are introduced and as those services change, the demand to modify the access control component is likely to outgrow the access control team's capacity to roll out changes in time.

For organizations that wish to prioritize control and security it may be reasonable to trade the speed of change for improved system safety and security. However, if you want to optimize for speed of implementation you'll need to take a different decentralized approach.

Decentralized controls

The implication here is that the individual microservice teams will need to manage an infrastructure that includes security mechanisms that are bounded to the service itself. The organization may standardize on the particular components and libraries that are to be used in every microservice, but it will be the teams themselves that are responsible for implementing security components and configuring them accordingly. It naturally follows that someone on the team must also take on the role of becoming the security expert for the service.

Contextual controls
A third approach that an organization can take is to define subsystems within the microservice architecture. Each subsystem may contain multiple services and their services within the subsystem are able to share common resources such as access control. Again, the organization may mandate the nature and requirement for these security components to be in place, but it is up to a subsystem service team to own and manage the configuration for the security component.

Security will always be an important design consideration for your microservice system. Even the absence of security is an implicit trade-off. While decisions about *how* and *what* to secure will be dependent on the risk profile of your organization and nature of the application you are building, the decision about *who* will manage the security implementation and *where* it will be implemented will have a big impact on your ability to optimize for the system behavior that you want.

Designing services that may be used by all other services in the system in itself is not a problem. A commonly used service that is resilient, reliable, and available will not impede the efforts of the rest of the service teams in the system. However, a commonly used service becomes a problem if the cost of implementing, configuring, and changing it becomes so high that it reduces the ability for service teams to make changes to the system.

Services Guidance

In a microservice system, the services form the atomic building blocks from which the entire organism is built. The following are some additional questions and issues we've identified when implementing well-designed microservices and APIs.

Should all microservices be coded in the same programming language?

The short answer is "no." The internal language of the component is not as important as the external interface—the API—of that component. As long as two components can use the same network protocols to exchange messages in an agreed-upon format using shared terms, the programming language used to accomplish all this is not important.

At the same time, many companies we talked to constrained the number of languages supported in the organization in order to simplify support and training. While a polyglot environment has advantages, too many languages results in added nonessential complexity system developers and maintainers need to deal with.

What do I do about orphaned components?

Over the life of a microservice implementation teams will come and go, and sometimes a team might disband and this can result in an "orphaned" microservice. It's not a good idea to just let a service run along without someone to care for it. As Martin Fowler points out in "Products not Projects" (*http://martinfowler.com/articles/micro services.html*), "ownership" is an important organizational aspect of microservices.

When a team is about to disband, that team needs to designate a new "owner" of the microservice component. This might be one of the existing team members ("OK, I'll take responsibility for it"). It might be some other team that is willing to take care of it. Or it might be someone who has taken on the special role of caring for "orphaned" services. But someone needs to be designated as the "owner."

It's not safe to allow orphaned services to run in your infrastructure.

Summary

It is unlikely that the microservice system you design will be exactly like the ones that Amazon, Netflix, SoundCloud, or any of the other companies you may have heard do microservices *correctly*. Since there isn't a formal definition for microservices, it's easy enough for you to call whatever you do a microservice architecture. What you call your system is relatively unimportant. But if your goal is to improve the changeability and adaptability of your system, following some of the principles we've outlined throughout this book will help get you there.

In this chapter we've outlined some methods for dealing with some of the challenges that many implementers face when introducing the microservice style to their organizations. But it is important that you decide if the benefits of a microservice system outweigh the cost of changes that will be required to get there. It's unlikely that every organization needs to build applications in the microservices way. This doesn't mean that you can't take advantage of innovative tools—you can use Docker containers without rearchitecting your application and you can introduce modular services without redesigning your team structure. But to really take advantage of this adaptive way of building applications, you'll need to eventually address all of the system components.

CHAPTER 8

Epilogue

The best software architecture "knows" what changes often and makes that easy.

—Paul Clements, author of *Software Architecture in Practice*

While this book bears the title *microservice architecture*, you have likely noticed that the central theme has been *change*. Specifically, we've focused on designing systems that make change easier.

When we work in a business environment where the goals and processes change frequently, our software architecture needs to reflect that. When it doesn't, the gap between business practice and system functionality widens and we call that "technical debt." On the other hand, when you engineer your system to support change safely—to allow replacing small interoperable parts without having to rebuild the entire system—then you're making change easier and avoiding that widening gap between practice and code.

Microservices are the small interoperable parts and microservice architecture is the engineering practice that can make change easier. The process of working along the path from your current architectural state and the desired future state where you can harmonize the speed of change with the need for system safety is what we call the microservices way.

Another key point to keep in mind is that there is no "all done" moment, that instant when you'll have everything in place, just the way you like it all running along without the need for modification. This need for constant change is not a "bug" in the way your software is engineered or implemented—it's a *feature* of a vital, viable information system. While there may be times when things tend to calm down or seem to run fairly quietly, they're not likely to last very long.

As someone responsible for making sure IT practices keep in alignment with business goals and objectives, you'll find lots of opportunity for "wins," but they might look a bit different than you'd expect. For example, a "win" is when you release refactored updates to core services without anyone even noticing. Or you complete a multiyear migration from one data-storage system to another. Or you learn that other teams in the company are now releasing customer-facing applications at a speed not previously thought possible. If you're lucky, someone will remember that all this was possible because of the work you've been doing all along.

As you've seen from our examples, you don't need to transform your organization, culture, and processes all in one "big bang." There are lots of small moves you can implement as you learn from each attempt and gain experience in the microservices way. And, you'll need all that experience as you face new challenges to adapt what you've built today to meet the unique goals and requirements of the future. Hopefully, the descriptions, models, and guidance we've collected here can give you a set of *tools* you can use to improve your organization's software system starting today and well into the future.

As we mentioned at the outset, we don't think it's important to agree upon a universal definition for the term "microservice." We don't even expect the current popularity of the term to last long. However, the principles that make microservices special—things like immutability and modularity, speed and safety, resilience, and agility—are well-known and lasting values. Technology advancements are already occurring as we write this book. The world around us is changing. Concepts such as serverless architectures, automated transport, virtual reality, and adaptive intelligent programs are all generating interest. We can't predict the future, and any of these technological or social changes could have a profound impact on the industry we share. That may mean that the range and types of tools available in the future may change in profound ways. These potential changes can alter the implementation details and processes you use to meet your goals but the underlying principles will stay the same.

And, even with all the possibilities of rapid change ahead, we think the microservices way of developing software—the harmonic balance of speed and safety at scale—will be valuable to you far into the future. So, when technology, society, and businesses change around you, you can use *the way* to identify the best of the new principles and patterns that will inevitably emerge from these important changes. That means you have the opportunity to embrace change and more easily adapt to new ways of designing, building, and managing the information systems of the future.

Nothing endures but change.

—Heraclitus

Microservice Architecture Reading List

There are a number of great resources out there for learning about microservice architecture, many of which helped to shape this book. This appendix collects and classifies the authors' favorites.

Microservices 101

These materials are the best place to start learning about microservices and microservice architecture:

- Lewis, James, and Martin Fowler. "Microservices: A Definition of This New Architectural Term" (*http://martinfowler.com/articles/microservices.html*), March 25, 2014.

- Miller, Matt. "Innovate or Die: The Rise of Microservices" (*http://blogs.wsj.com/cio/2015/10/05/innovate-or-die-the-rise-of-microservices/*). *The Wall Street Journal*, October 5, 2015.

- Newman, Sam. *Building Microservices* (*http://bit.ly/building-microservices*). O'Reilly Media, 2015.

Best Practices

These resources provide guidance on what to do—and what not to do—when it comes to implementing a microservice architecture:

- Alagarasan, Vijay. "Seven Microservices Anti-patterns" (*http://www.infoq.com/articles/seven-uservices-antipatterns*), August 24, 2015.

- Cockcroft, Adrian. "State of the Art in Microservices" (*http://www.slideshare.net/ adriancockcroft/dockercon-state-of-the-art-in-microservices*), December 4, 2014.

- Fowler, Martin. "Microservice Prerequisites" (*http://martinfowler.com/bliki/Micro servicePrerequisites.html*), August 28, 2014.

- Fowler, Martin. "Microservice Tradeoffs" (*http://martinfowler.com/articles/ microservice-trade-offs.html*), July 1, 2015.

- Humble, Jez. "Four Principles of Low-Risk Software Release" (*http://www.infor mit.com/articles/article.aspx?p=1833567*), February 16, 2012.

- Humble, Jez, Chris Read, and Dan North. "The Deployment Production Line" (*http://dl.acm.org/citation.cfm?id=1155519*). In *Proceedings of the conference on AGILE 2006*, 113–118. IEEE Computer Society.

- Kniberg, Henrik, and Anders Ivarsson. "Scaling Agile at Spotify" (*https://dl.drop boxusercontent.com/u/1018963/Articles/SpotifyScaling.pdf*), October 2012.

- Vasters, Clemens. "Sagas" (*http://vasters.com/clemensv/2012/09/01/Sagas.aspx*), September 1, 2012.

- Wootton, Benjamin. "Microservices are Not a Free Lunch" (*http://highscalabil ity.com/blog/2014/4/8/microservices-not-a-free-lunch.html*), April 8, 2014.

Example Implementations

The following articles include overviews and insight from real-life microservice implementations:

- Amazon Web Services (*https://queue.acm.org/detail.cfm?id=1142065*)

- Autoscout24 (*http://www.infoq.com/news/2016/02/autoscout-microservices*)

- CA Technologies (Rally) (*https://www.rallydev.com/blog/engineering/introduction- microservices-0*)

- Disney (*http://www.computerworld.com/article/2999969/application- development/modular-software-creates-agility-and-complexity.html*)

- Gilt

  — *http://www.infoq.com/presentations/microservices-dependencies*

  — *http://www.infoq.com/news/2015/04/scaling-microservices-gilt*

- ITV (*https://skillsmatter.com/skillscasts/6186-domain-service-aggregators-a- structured-approach-to-microservice-composition*)

- Jet.com (*http://tech.just-eat.com/2016/03/08/tech-talk-rachel-reese-jet-com- microservices-in-the-real-world/*)

- Netflix

- *http://techblog.netflix.com/2015/01/netflixs-viewing-data-how-we-know-where.html*
- *https://yow.eventer.com/yow-2013-1080/cloud-native-architecture-at-netflix-by-adrian-cockcroft-1364*

- Nike (*http://www.zdnet.com/article/how-nike-thinks-about-app-development-lots-of-micro-services/*)
- SoundCloud
  - *https://www.thoughtworks.com/insights/blog/bff-soundcloud*
  - *http://www.infoq.com/articles/microservices-evolution-soundcloud*
  - *http://philcalcado.com/2015/09/08/how_we_ended_up_with_microservices.html*
- Spotify (*https://www.infoq.com/news/2015/12/microservices-spotify*)
- Trinity Mirror Group (*http://www.computerweekly.com/news/4500271221/Trinity-Mirror-Group-uses-cloud-and-performance-monitoring-to-boost-website-users-experience*)

Foundations

The last set of resources includes the historical foundations for microservice architecture:

- Arthur, W. Brian. *The Nature of Technology* (*http://tuvalu.santafe.edu/%7Ewbarthur/thenatureoftechnology.htm*). Simon & Schuster, 2009.
- Brooks, Fred. "No Silver Bullet" (*http://worrydream.com/refs/Brooks-NoSilverBullet.pdf*). Reproduced from *The Mythical Man-Month, Anniversary edition*, Addison-Wesley, 1995.
- Conway, Mel. "Conway's Law" (*http://www.melconway.com/Home/Conways_Law.html*), accessed May 25, 2016.
- Evans, Eric. *Domain-Driven Design: Tackling Complexity in the Heart of Software*. Prentice-Hall, 2003.
- Fielding, Roy. "Architectural Styles and the Design of Network-based Software Architectures" (*https://www.ics.uci.edu/~fielding/pubs/dissertation/top.htm*). PhD diss., University of California, Irvine, 2000.
- Feldman, Stuart. "A Conversation with Alan Kay" (*http://queue.acm.org/detail.cfm?id=1039523*). *Queue* 2(2004): 20–30.
- Mintzberg, Henry. *Structure in Fives: Designing Effective Organizations* (*http://www.mintzberg.org/books/structure-5s-designing-effective-organizations*). Pearson, 1992.

- Morgan, Gareth. *Images of Organization* (*https://us.sagepub.com/en-us/nam/images-of-organization/book229704*). SAGE Publishing, 2007.

- Parnas, David. "On the Criteria to Be Used in Decomposing Systems Into Modules" (*https://www.cs.umd.edu/class/spring2003/cmsc838p/Design/criteria.pdf*). *Communications of the ACM* 15(1972): 1053–1058.

- Poppendieck, Mary. "The New New Software Development Game" (*http://www.ustream.tv/recorded/61477219/theater*), Craft Conference video, April 2015.

- Ries, Eric. *The Lean Startup* (*http://theleanstartup.com/book*). Crown Business, 2011.

Index

A
adaptability, change and, 29
Agile Manifesto, 65
Air Force, US, 23
alerting, 101
Allspaw, John
    on monitoring, 44
Amazon
    and size of teams at, 56
    automated testing of code, 51
Amazon machine images (AMIs), 53
Amazon Web Services, 13, 98
antifragility, 45
API design
    and output standardization, 32
    hypermedia-driven implementation, 68-70
    message-oriented implementation, 67
    standardization trade-offs, 33
API gateway, 98-101
    routing, 101
    security, 98
    transformation and orchestration, 99-101
architectural policy services, 52
Arthur, W. Brian
    on modularity, 17
asynchronous message-passing, 80
automated testing, 44
autonomy of microservices teams, 8
averages, drawbacks as basis for design, 23

B
batch-size reduction, 65
Bezos, Jeff
    on size of teams at Amazon, 56

blue-green deployment, 44
boundaries
    and batch-size reduction, 65
    and bounded contexts, 64
    and domain-driven design, 62
    in service design, 62-66
    ubiquitous language, 66
bounded contexts, 64
    and business context, 66
    optimal size of, 66
Brooks, Fred
    and Conway's Law, 55
    on team size and communication overhead, 56
business context, bounded context and, 66

C
Cai, Beier
    on efficiency benefits of microservice, 14
    on governance at Hootsuite, 60
Calçado, Phil
    and value stream mapping, 109
    efficiency benefits of microservice, 15
    on microservices, 3
capabilities, data vs., 70
capabilities-oriented design, 71
change
    centrality to microservice architecture, 117
    embracing, 29
    introducing, 109-110
    safety of, 9
    speed of, 9
    Vision Zero and, 1
chaos, tolerance for, 58

systems design, 25-39
    and operations (see operational management)
    and systems approach to microservices, 25-33
    foundation for, 41-58
    goals, 42
    microservice system design model, 27
    microservices design process, 33-38

T

teams
    alignment, 56
    autonomy of, 8
    organizational design, 28
    size of, 56
technical debt, 37, 106
testing, automated, 44
tight coupling
    data sharing and, 84
    waterfall approach and, 112
time, as essential element in microservice system, 29
tools
    building, 48
    choosing, 28
    practical guidance for, 111
traffic systems, 1
transformation
    API gateway, 99-101
    as unending process, 106
Trenaman, Adrian
    on microservice architecture at Gilt, 14
Twitter

Decider configuration tool, 53
Zipkin, 54

U

ubiquitous language, 66
Unix, 46
Urban, Steve
    on team leadership at Netflix, 57
US Air Force, 23

V

value proposition, 13-21
    architecture benefits, 13-15
    business value, 15-16
    goal-oriented, layered approach, 17-19
value stream mapping, 109
Vernon, Vaughn
    on bounded context, 66
virtual machines (VMs), 50
visibility, runtime, 44
Vision Zero, 1
Vogels, Werner
    on Amazon Web Services architecture, 13
    on running what you build, 52

Y

Young, Greg
    on event sourcing, 72
Yourdon, Edward
    on cohesive architecture, 18

Z

Zipkin, 54

About the Authors

Irakli Nadareishvili is CTO and cofounder of a New York health tech startup Refer-Well. At any given time he can be found designing and implementing APIs, discussing distributed systems architecture, and expressing opinions about product management. Prior to ReferWell, Irakli held leadership roles at the API Academy of CA Technologies and NPR. Irakli is highly involved in the startup community and has spent over a decade in Washington, DC building innovative products for media companies and government and international organizations, while also being an active open source contributor and advocate.

Ronnie Mitra is the Director of Design at CA's API Academy, and is focused on helping people design better distributed systems. He travels around the world, helping organizations adopt a design-centric approach to interface design and a system-centric approach to application architecture.

Matt McLarty is Vice President of the API Academy at CA Technologies. The API Academy helps companies thrive in the digital economy by providing expert guidance on strategy, architecture, and design for APIs.

In his role of Director of Architecture for the API Academy, **Mike Amundsen** heads up the API Architecture and Design Practice in North America. He is responsible for working with companies to provide insight on how best to capitalize on the myriad opportunities APIs present to both consumers and the enterprise.

Amundsen has authored numerous books and papers on programming over the last 15 years.

Colophon

The animal on the cover of *Microservice Architecture* is a cowry snail, an ocean-dwelling mollusk of the *Cypraeidae* family, found worldwide in tropical waters. There are many species of different sizes and shell patterns, but all possess a very rounded shell with a smooth glossy exterior. The texture of these shells is similar to porcelain, which itself was named after the Italian term for these snails: *porcellana*. Cowrie shells have historically been used as currency in several world cultures, and are still popular in jewelry and decoration.

The shell of a cowry snail is also distinctive for its narrow toothed opening. It's very difficult for predators to get into, though some species (such as certain octopi and carnivorous snails of the cone family) attack by injecting venom directly into the cowry's flesh.

Cowry snails themselves primarily feed on algae, but also eat sea sponges. They are most active at night. During the day, the snails hide inside coral reefs or beneath rocks. The part of the snail visible outside the shell is the mantle, a muscular fringed appendage that not only provides locomotion but excretes calcium carbonate, the substance that gradually builds up and maintains the shell around the animal.

Many of the animals on O'Reilly covers are endangered; all of them are important to the world. To learn more about how you can help, go to *animals.oreilly.com*.

The cover image is from *Beauties of Land and Sea*. The cover fonts are URW Typewriter and Guardian Sans. The text font is Adobe Minion Pro; the heading font is Adobe Myriad Condensed; and the code font is Dalton Maag's Ubuntu Mono.

Get even more for your money.

Join the O'Reilly Community, and register the O'Reilly books you own. It's free, and you'll get:

- $4.99 ebook upgrade offer
- 40% upgrade offer on O'Reilly print books
- Membership discounts on books and events
- Free lifetime updates to ebooks and videos
- Multiple ebook formats, DRM FREE
- Participation in the O'Reilly community
- Newsletters
- Account management
- 100% Satisfaction Guarantee

Signing up is easy:

1. Go to: oreilly.com/go/register
2. Create an O'Reilly login.
3. Provide your address.
4. Register your books.

Note: English-language books only

To order books online:
oreilly.com/store

For questions about products or an order:
orders@oreilly.com

To sign up to get topic-specific email announcements and/or news about upcoming books, conferences, special offers, and new technologies:
elists@oreilly.com

For technical questions about book content:
booktech@oreilly.com

To submit new book proposals to our editors:
proposals@oreilly.com

O'Reilly books are available in multiple DRM-free ebook formats. For more information:
oreilly.com/ebooks

O'REILLY®

©2014 O'Reilly Media, Inc. O'Reilly logo is a registered trademark of O'Reilly Media, Inc. 14373

Milton Keynes UK
Ingram Content Group UK Ltd.
UKHW031829290823
427704UK00007B/278